Guiding Gifted Students With Engaging Books

Guiding Gifted Students With Engaging Books supports teachers and counselors in facilitating book discussions designed to guide bright young people to self-understanding through high-quality literature. This exciting resource:

- Covers social-emotional issues in the lives of gifted students.
- Features examples of lessons and menus of discussion questions for successful book discussions alongside enrichment activities to extend students' learning.
- Includes an annotated bibliography of children's and young adult books ideal for social-emotional learning.

Engaging lessons and activities support learners as they process their feelings regarding issues highlighted in the selected books and class discussion. The book examines this approach with whole classrooms, as well as with small groups of students, and features considerations for special populations of gifted students, including twice-exceptional students, culturally diverse students, and children and teens facing serious adversity in their lives.

Thomas P. Hébert is Professor of Gifted and Talented Education in the College of Education at the University of South Carolina, USA. He has more than a decade of K-12 classroom experience working with gifted students and 25 years in higher education training graduate students and educators in gifted education.

Guiding Gifted Students With Engaging Books

A Teacher's Guide to Social-Emotional
Learning Through Reading and Reflection

Thomas P. Hébert

 Routledge
Taylor & Francis Group

NEW YORK AND LONDON

Cover image: © Shutterstock

First published 2022
by Routledge
605 Third Avenue, New York, NY 10158

and by Routledge
4 Park Square, Milton Park, Abingdon, Oxon, OX14 4RN

Routledge is an imprint of the Taylor & Francis Group, an informa business

Library of Congress Cataloging-in-Publication Data
Names: Hébert, Thomas Paul, author.
Title: Guiding gifted students with engaging books: a teacher's guide to social-emotional learning through reading and reflection/Thomas P. Hébert.
Description: New York, NY: Routledge, 2022. | Includes bibliographical references.
Identifiers: LCCN 2021044572 (print) | LCCN 2021044573 (ebook) | ISBN 9781032144924 (hardback) | ISBN 9781646321940 (paperback) | ISBN 9781003235408 (ebook)
Subjects: LCSH: Gifted children–Education–Psychological aspects. | Affective education. | Reflective learning. | Children's literature–Study and teaching. | Children–Books and reading.
Classification: LCC LC3993.2 .H43 2022 (print) | LCC LC3993.2 (ebook) | DDC 371.95–dc23/eng/20211006
LC record available at https://lccn.loc.gov/2021044572
LC ebook record available at https://lccn.loc.gov/2021044573

ISBN: 978-1-032-14492-4 (hbk)
ISBN: 978-1-64632-194-0 (pbk)
ISBN: 978-1-003-23540-8 (ebk)

DOI: 10.4324/9781003235408

Typeset in Optima
by Deanta Global Publishing Services, Chennai, India

To former gifted students who shared their social and emotional lives with me.

Contents

Acknowledgments

I first want to thank my dear friend and colleague Susan Baum for introducing me to the concept of guiding gifted students through literature. I especially want to thank Lacy Compton and Katy McDowall for their encouragement of this book. Their thoughtful guidance supported me throughout my writing process. I am grateful to Susannah Richards for sharing her passion for children's literature with me and recommending many of her favorite books.

Guiding Gifted Students to Self-Understanding
The Process

Jon Harris spent many of his summers in New England reading in his backyard. As a young teen, he was the bookworm in his family. While his younger brother spent his days involved in sports, Jon was content to relax in a lawn chair under the family's maple trees and devour good books. On Saturday mornings, he typically walked downtown to the local public library to return books and acquire several new titles for the upcoming week. As a seventh grader, Jon enjoyed browsing through the library's collection and he especially enjoyed visiting with a special friend who worked there. Elizabeth Cunningham, known as "Tizz," was a sophomore in high school who worked weekends in the children's room of the library. Jon was captivated by her cool nickname, friendly smile, and long blonde hair. Though his parents were pleased that he was making weekly trips to the library, Jon figured they didn't need to know about his growing crush for the "older woman" in his life.

One Saturday, Tizz took a look at the books Jon had decided on for the week and suggested a novel that she thought he might enjoy. When she mentioned that the author used tawdry language throughout the text, Jon became more intrigued. Pleased that his older friend thought he was sophisticated enough to handle the novel, he added it to his pile for checking out.

When Jon returned home to his lawn chair in the backyard, he began reading the novel Tizz had recommended. He quickly became immersed in the coming-of-age story of another teenager who was unhappy with his adolescent life and the world around him. The protagonist in the story was questioning so much about society and raising many existential questions that plagued him. Jon silently thought that the main character in this novel was speaking directly to him. He identified with his challenges and could appreciate his angst. He devoured the novel within two days and spent

DOI: 10.4324/9781003235408-1

the remainder of the week reflecting on the story. As he thought about the novel, he felt a sense of relief. The protagonist in the novel expressed some of the very thoughts and feelings that Jon was experiencing as an adolescent. As a result, he realized that he was not alone with his teenage worries and frustrations and that was reassuring. For Jon, it was a relief to know that other 13-year-olds had the same concerns. His experience with the book enabled him to reflect on his own situation as an adolescent and continue his search for self-understanding.

The Power of Books

In the midst of the Coronavirus pandemic, I received a scholarly electronic flyer from the University of Toronto Press that impressed me. The first two sentences read, "As the world around us undergoes profound transformation, books remain constant. They are a source of wisdom, comfort, connection, and wonder" (UTP, 2020). I have reflected on this passage many times throughout the process of writing this book. I believe it succinctly captures a significant understanding of the power of literature and reminds us of how books may serve as influential instruments in shaping lives. Over 50 years ago, Lejeune (1969), a scholar of counseling psychology, addressed the phenomenon of influential books and how they serve many purposes in the lives of young people. In his reflections, Lejeune (1969) noted that books can help to identify, extend, and intensify the interests of children. He believed that books provide young people an awareness of themselves and others and may offer children an emotional release. He maintained that books induce curiosity and reflective thinking and provide opportunities for re-examining values. In addition to offering pure enjoyment and entertainment, he indicated that books provided young people connections to their culture. He concluded that nothing children learn can compare with the love of books.

Guiding Gifted Students through Literature

Jon's connection to the poignant young adult novel is consistent with LeJeune's belief in the power of books; however, his experience may have been more meaningful if he had enjoyed the opportunity to discuss the book with others who reflected on insights gained from the author. Jon's experience with his novel may be referred to as bibliotherapy, defined as the use of reading to produce affective change and personality growth and development (Lenkowsky, 1987). Another seminal definition is Lundsteen's (1972): "getting the right book to the right child at the right time about the right problem" (p. 505). With educators and graduate students enrolled in my gifted education courses, I describe the approach as "guiding gifted young people to self-understanding through literature." In my work with teachers and young scholars, I ask them to think about how educators and counselors can transfer Jon's experience to classrooms and extend the reflection of students as they engage in meaningful book conversations with other readers.

I am reluctant to use the term bibliotherapy simply because I do not want to raise concerns among parents and administrators that I am doing something I am not qualified to do as a classroom teacher. I am not a therapist; however, as a practitioner, I can facilitate good discussions with children and teens about good books. In doing so, I can help them draw parallels between their experiences and those of the main characters in the literature we read together. I can also help them listen to their classroom peers as they share their feelings about personal experiences related to the focus of the book. This approach is simply an attempt to help young people understand themselves and cope with problems by providing literature relevant to their personal situations and developmental needs at appropriate times.

Cross (2004) highlighted the wide range of needs that gifted students may have and the potential roles that different groups of adults play in supporting them. In doing so, he created a "continuum of psychological services" that included the broadest area of need to the most focused. He delineated the following: Advising – Guidance – Counseling – Therapy – Psychopharmacology (p. 2).

The approach I am describing in this book is categorized as *guidance* on the Cross continuum and is consistent with the conceptual framework known as social and emotional learning (Weissberg et al., 2015). Schools that incorporate social and emotional learning implement practices that help children acquire the competencies to understand and manage emotions, establish and achieve positive goals, feel and show caring and concern for others, establish and build positive relationships, and make responsible decisions in life. The practice of teachers and counselors facilitating discussions that focus on high-quality literature and address affective concerns is an efficient strategy for infusing social and emotional learning in order to develop self-awareness, self-management, social awareness, relationship skills, and responsible decision making (Weissberg et al., 2015) in young people.

Discussions centered on engaging books enable teachers and counselors to guide students in thinking through issues in their lives that are developmental – a part of the natural process of growing up. I want to emphasize this important term. *Developmental* challenges are those that all children encounter, including gifted kids, and include concerns such as searching for and maintaining friendships, believing in self, dealing with parental and teacher expectations, determining healthy self-expectations, and coping with peer pressure.

In conducting book discussions in classrooms, I focus on these developmental issues that many gifted students experience – perhaps more intensely and in different ways – and I reserve more serious concerns, the types I would label "grit your teeth issues" for counselors. Teachers of gifted students using this approach believe that reading can influence thinking and behavior, and that guided discussions about selected books can focus on the specific needs of students. Such an approach attempts to address the concerns of young people before these concerns become problems, providing needed information and understanding for facing the challenges of adolescence.

Developmental Issues to Address in School Settings

In my work in summer institutes in gifted education, I have listened to teachers. I have had the opportunity to survey several groups of educators to determine particular concerns they believed were appropriate to address with gifted students implementing this approach in schools (Hébert, 2018). With more emotionally laden or controversial issues the teachers indicated that they would reach for the support of school counselors in their settings. Following my thematic analysis of their responses, the following issues were those that elementary teachers felt comfortable handling in open class discussions:

- parental expectations;
- relationships with parents and siblings;

- celebrating families;
- finding and building authentic friendships;
- peer group pressure;
- celebrating individual differences;
- appreciating diversity;
- developing empathy;
- being comfortable with one's personal creativity;
- developing one's talents;
- juggling academics and athletics;
- dealing with disappointments;
- coping with stress and anxiety; and
- celebrating one's uniqueness.

I also surveyed middle and high school teachers regarding this question (Hébert, 2019). The responses of the secondary educators were similar and included the following:

- self-expectations, parental expectations, and peer expectations;
- being overwhelmed by competing expectations;
- relationships with parents and siblings;
- relationships with teachers;
- finding authentic friendships;
- understanding introversion and extraversion;
- peer pressure;
- underachievement;
- competition;
- developing courage;
- developing resilience;
- multipotentiality;
- heightened emotional intensity;
- understanding and appreciating individual value systems;
- appreciating diversity;
- celebrating individual creativity;
- gender role expectations;
- nonconformity;
- perfectionism;
- coping with stress;
- the challenges of twice-exceptionality;

- striving for self-actualization;
- identity development;
- believing in self;
- career explorations; and
- future lifestyle expectations.

From those surveys and in my conversations with K-12 educators and counselors, I was assured that many professionals believe that having meaningful discussions through good books has tremendous potential for addressing the developmental concerns of gifted students.

In her seminal work, *Some of My Best Friends are Books*, Judith Halsted (2009) highlighted particular qualities or characteristics of individuals who effectively facilitate discussions of social and emotional issues with young people:

- Maturity: A self-awareness, self-acceptance, and tolerance of others
- Integrity: A respect for self and others that enables an individual to avoid exploitation of emotions
- Responsibility: An attitude of responsiveness as well as a willingness to guide children and teens through potentially difficult conversations
- Adaptability: The ability to adjust plans to meet the needs of a group at any moment and to allow the participants to enjoy their own interpretations (p. 111)

In addition to these characteristics, she indicated that teachers and counselors who engage in this work must acquire the following "therapeutic attitudes" (p. 111):

- Empathy: The ability to understand another person's feelings
- Respect: The recognition of the value of another person's feelings and the appreciation of his or her inherent worth and uniqueness
- Genuineness: Sincerity, openness, spontaneity, awareness, and acceptance of one's own inner experiences

Additionally, Halsted (2009) noted that individuals who lead discussion groups using literature with gifted students should be well versed in a variety of discussion techniques, know and enjoy high-quality children's literature, have a good understanding of adolescent development in general, and gifted children in particular, have the trust of the young people with whom they are working, and be comfortable with listening to them closely.

Understanding the Therapeutic Process

Jon's appreciation of the poignant young adult novel in his summer reading serves as an inspirational example of the power of books and should inspire educators and counselors in supporting students like Jon by engaging in high-quality literature. The experience of young people benefitting from reading literature and engaging in a book discussion that addresses social and emotional concerns involves several stages: *identification, catharsis, insight,* and *universalization* (Halsted, 2009; Hébert & Kent, 2000). The therapeutic experience begins when young people pick up a book and discover characters very much like themselves. This interaction is known as *identification,* and the more gifted students have in common with the people they meet in their books, the closer the identification process. With that identification comes the second stage – a sense of tension relief, or *catharsis,* an emotional feeling that lets children and teens know that they are not alone in facing their problems. As they enjoy a story, they learn vicariously through the book's characters. They gain new ways of examining troublesome issues, and *insight* evolves – the third stage of the process. With this new insight, changed behavior may occur as they begin to consider how to address their real-life situations that are similar to those experienced by the characters in the books. With the support of the teacher or counselor leading the discussion, the next stage – *universalization* – can occur in which participants reach the recognition that their difficulties and sense of difference are not theirs alone (Halsted, 2009). By asking questions that focus on identification with a character, then on the problematic situation, how the story character handled it, the feelings stirred within the reader, and lastly, on the ways in which the book connects with the reader's own life, the facilitator is able to help students recognize the *universalization* – the "Aha!" moment when students see that we are *all* in this experience of living life together. Moreover, I believe that if the adult facilitating the conversation does an effective job with the group and takes time in the discussion to have participants generate a variety of coping strategies to apply to a problematic situation the next time they encounter it, then the final component of the process – *application* – will have been reached.

7

Preparing a Lesson

In selecting high-quality literature, teachers can consider the suggestions of Halsted (2009), who recommends searching for books that offer situations that evoke emotions and stories that offer alternatives and characters with whom the readers can identify. In addition, teachers must recognize that all young people will need books that help them understand the multicultural nature of the world in which they live, their place in that world, and their connection to all other humans. In her seminal work, Dr. Rudine Sims Bishop (1990) reminded educators of their influential roles in shaping the lives of the children they teach, and this is especially true when making selections of literature featured in their classrooms. As a children's literature enthusiast, she delivered that message metaphorically:

> Books are sometimes windows, offering views of worlds that may be real or imagined, familiar or strange. The windows are also sliding glass doors, and readers have only to walk through in imagination to become part of whatever world has been created and recreated by the author. When lighting conditions are just right, however, a window can also be a mirror. Literature transforms human experience and reflects it back to us, and in that reflection we can see our own lives and experiences as part of the larger human experience. Reading, then, becomes a means of self-affirmation, and readers often seek their mirrors in books.

(p ix–xi)

This passage emphasizes the relationship and the experience the reader may have with literature. We are reminded of Jon Harris and see how his experience with the novel he read was clearly that of a mirror. Scholars in gifted education maintain this approach of providing for diverse populations of students is critical (Abellán-Pagnani & Hébert, 2013; Fears-Floyd & Hébert, 2010; Ford, 2000). Teachers and counselors will want to guarantee the books they select are reflective of all readers and include literature that appropriately affirms the identities of all young people from various racial, ethnic, religious, and socioeconomic backgrounds and lifestyles (Richards, 2021).

Along with paying attention to the selection of an appropriate book, teachers and counselors facilitating a lesson must consider planning and preparation before beginning the session. In addition to reading the entire book, the facilitator should prepare an extensive menu of discussion questions crafted in such a way that the students involved in the discussion will feel comfortable sharing their own experiences with the emotional or difficult issues presented in the book. Facilitators begin the conversation with nonthreatening questions to establish a comfort level before delving into follow-up questions that address more sensitive issues central to the personal lives of the children and teens involved in the discussion. A sensitively designed menu of questions is necessary for a cathartic conversation that will lead to self-understanding. In addition to generating discussion questions to guide the conversation, educators implementing this approach have often found it useful to bookmark significant quotes from the text of the book that may be especially poignant, inspirational, or thought-provoking. Having these quotes ready at one's fingertips may come in handy when searching for an appropriate prompt for further discussion.

When teachers and counselors conduct discussions of thought-provoking or sensitive issues, the conversation may trigger emotional responses within the participants. Therefore, it is important that facilitators design and plan for follow-up activities that allow children and teens to process through their feelings. For example, there may be a student in the group who discovers that he self-disclosed more information than he had planned on in the group discussion and is struggling to figure out a way to protect his image in school. He may be somewhat "rattled" by that disclosure and may need some time to "chill" and think through how he might respond to questions from his friends. Follow-up activities should enable him to benefit from some "chill" time and enjoy continued conversation with the members of the group.

Teachers and counselors who facilitate discussion groups are responding to the needs of their students as they incorporate follow-up activities. Such activities might include creative writing, poetry, creative problem solving, journaling, writing song lyrics, writing raps, writing a letter or news article, technology, designing television commercials, role-playing interviews with the book's main character, holding a mock trial, creating a collage, cartooning and other art activities, or self-selected options for students to pursue individually (DeVries, et al., 2017; Hébert, 2020; Stambaugh, 2019).

As mentioned earlier, the follow-up activities should be enjoyable and provide time for introspection – time to reflect and "chill." In conducting the follow-up activities, I have discovered that the more enjoyable they are, the more effective they become. I emphasize enjoyable because I have found that as young people are engaged in something fun, they are more apt to continue discussion among themselves about the issues talked about in the group. As they engage in the activities, the students continue to provide each other with supportive feedback. For example, a teacher facilitates a book discussion on bullying, and as the students are working, she overhears comments such as, "Seth, I didn't know that Matt McGillicuddy used to pick on you, too, back in second grade. It really made me feel better to hear that I wasn't the only kid he bullied. That dude was mean!"

I have also learned that effective follow-up activities can be either collaborative or private. Providing students a choice of working in groups or alone addresses individual learning styles. This consideration may be critical to students who tend toward introversion as these opportunities may help them integrate new ideas gleaned in the discussion with their own private thoughts about the book (Halsted, 2009). Moreover, I have discovered that when discussions involve students engaging in serious self-disclosure, private journaling as a follow-up activity provides time to "process" their feelings. I have come to believe that the follow-up activities are as important as the group discussion, and I have found that the more hands-on the follow-up activity, the more boys will talk. Engaging in hands-on activity is critical for young men to feel more comfortable in discussing their feelings (Hébert, 2017). Girls seem to have fewer problems with talking about anything related to emotions. With these points considered, guided discussions centered on affective concerns can be enjoyable while providing a time for significant introspection (Hébert, 2020).

Options to Consider

Conducting discussions centered on social and emotional development through good books can happen in a variety of ways. In the chapters that follow I invite my readers to enjoy different scenarios that highlight suggested approaches, keeping in mind that gifted students are present in each classroom described. In Chapter 2, a regular elementary classroom teacher begins the school year with her plan for creating a supportive classroom environment and decides to infuse several affirming picture books to welcome her students. Chapter 3 features a gifted education teacher who is concerned about an issue that is often evident in highly able children and teens. She is worried about the perfectionistic behaviors of her students and decides to address this issue in her gifted education classroom – a setting she believes is most appropriate for comfortable conversation on a rather sensitive issue. In Chapter 4, we meet a high school honors English teacher who sees a need to address identity development in gifted teens and infuses this approach through the literary options he provides his students. In Chapter 5, a gifted education teacher and a learning disabilities specialist collaborate in designing an intervention for twice-exceptional students. Chapter 6 highlights a collaborative approach in which a classroom teacher reaches out to a school counselor to support her in delivering lessons that address resilience and overcoming adversity. The final scenario in Chapter 7 provides an example of a school counselor who designs a timely intervention for a special population of students – gifted Black boys, incorporating picture books and young adult novels that focus on the challenges these young men face. Throughout the chapters, I provide my readers with sample lesson plans that include discussion questions and follow-up activities to be used with the books highlighted in each scenario.

A Wealth of Resources

In selecting high-quality literature to use with this approach, teachers and counselors should remain mindful of the influence of books they select to explore with students. They have the responsibility of selecting books of great worth, those that provide rich metaphors and help readers understand themselves and others, and literature that connects to the emotional lives of children and teens. To support them in their search for high-quality books, I have included an annotated bibliography of literature appropriate for grades K-12 in the appendix. The collection includes picture books, chapter books, and young adult novels that can be used to address social and emotional development. Before embarking on their work with book discussions, teachers and counselors will need to read the books from cover to cover. Young adult novels may include mature themes and language, therefore, it becomes critical for educators to read books thoroughly, and consider community values in order to make wise decisions regarding whether they are appropriate for use in a particular context.

I invite my readers to consider the variety of delivery options described in the chapters that follow, reflect on the approach that may be best for young people in different contexts, and encourage all to review the many wonderful books I have discovered for using with gifted children and teens.

Sofia Creates a Supportive Classroom Environment

Sofia Morales was excited about the upcoming school year at River Bluff Elementary School. She arrived in her classroom a week in advance of the opening day of school to begin preparing the room for her second graders. She investigated the inventory of technology in the room and was pleased to see new equipment waiting to be unpacked. After taking note of the number of bulletin boards she would have to decorate, she decided to wait on tackling that rather overwhelming task that morning. Instead, she was more interested in studying the school files on the children she would be teaching.

As she examined the files, she learned important information about the 22 children she would soon be meeting. Sofia recognized that her class would be a diverse population. She learned that she could anticipate working with children from a wide range of academic readiness levels. She scanned the records and noted that several of her students would be receiving services from the special education team as well as the bilingual education staff. Other children had been recommended by their first-grade teachers for screening for the gifted and talented education program. In studying the surnames of the children, she recognized that they represented a variety of racial and ethnic backgrounds. She also read documentation for a number of children who would be benefitting from the school district's free or reduced lunch program.

Sofia set aside the folders and began organizing the room. As she moved furniture, arranged her learning centers, and unpacked the new technology she reflected on the information she had gained from reading her students' files. She knew she would enjoy working with such a diverse group of children and began to think about how she might welcome her

DOI: 10.4324/9781003235408-2

students and establish a supportive classroom environment where individual differences in children were celebrated and a collaborative spirit became the culture of the classroom. She decided that she would spend some time in the evening examining some of her favorite teacher resource material for ideas.

Sofia left school that afternoon and decided to visit her neighborhood's new bookstore. She had shopped there earlier in the summer during the store's grand opening and was pleased to see such a large inventory of children's picture books. Sofia was happy to return to browsing through the collection again. As she browsed, she came upon one book that seemed like the perfect match for the diverse population of second graders that she would soon be meeting. Sofia decided to purchase Jacqueline Woodson's (2018) *The Day You Begin*. She smiled to herself as she thought about the raised eyebrow she would receive from her rather frugal husband when she arrived home with yet another children's book purchase, but she wasn't concerned about that conversation. She knew she would not have to spend time with teacher resource material, and she now looked forward to using her new book and preparing a lesson she would implement on the opening day of school.

The Day You Begin

Sofia appreciated Jacqueline Woodson's acknowledgment that there are many reasons that young children may feel different when they arrive in a new setting. It may be their appearance or how they talk, where they are from, or the food they eat. Sofia thought about what it takes for children who feel different to share their stories. As she read Jacqueline Woodson's work, she realized that it would serve as a wonderful pathway for children to discover the beauty in their own lives and share it with others. In doing so, they would be able to find someone a little bit like them. Sofia identified two important themes in *The Day You Begin* that would resonate with her students: finding a place where you belong and having the courage to be yourself. With the two overarching themes determined, she read through the text and generated the discussion questions she would use in guiding the conversation with her students. She also discovered some thought-provoking passages in the text that would serve as helpful prompts for discussion. She bookmarked those particular passages.

Sofia's Plan for the Session

Overarching themes:

- Finding a place where you belong
- Having the courage to be yourself

Discussion questions:

- What did the author mean when she began the story with this sentence: "There will be times when you walk into a room and no one there is quite like you"?
- Have you ever had a time when you walked into a room and no one there was quite like you? What did you notice? How did that make you feel? What did you do?
- When Rigoberto speaks up in class and the other students start to laugh, what does his teacher do? Why do you think she did that? How do you think Rigoberto feels about his teacher's comments?
- What does the teacher mean when she says that Rigoberto's "name and homeland sound like flowers blooming the first notes of a song"? Can you see that in your imagination? What does it look like?
- When the teacher asks the students about their summer vacation, what do we learn about them? What did their travel souvenirs tell you about their summer?
- What memories does Angelina have about her summer spent in the city watching out for her little sister? How do you think she feels?
- Why do you think Nadja wrinkled her nose when she saw what her best friend brought to school for lunch? Are there some special foods that you enjoy that other kids may not understand? How can you help them appreciate what you enjoy?
- Have you ever had a time when other children didn't choose you to join in their teams and play their games? How did you feel? What did you do? What advice would you give to other kids who may not be included?
- When children feel like the world seems like a place that they are standing outside of, how can they be brave? Have you ever felt that way? What did you do? What did you learn?

- Angelina finally shares her story of how she and her little sister spent their summer together in the city. What was the important message that she told the other children? What do you think of her message? If you could have a conversation with Angelina, what would you say to her?
- What does Rigoberto say to Angelina that helps him become her new friend? Why do you think that conversation was so important?
- The author of this beautiful book ends the story with this passage:

> This is the day you begin
> to find the places inside
> your laughter and your lunches,
> your books, your travel and your stories,
> where every new friend has something
> a little like you – and something else
> so fabulously not quite like you
> at all.

- What do you think she means? What is her message to us? How can we use this message this year in our classroom?

After generating her discussion questions, Sofia then prepared a menu of follow-up activities that her students would select from. Sofia realized that the activities would give time for the children to process their feelings about the significant messages delivered in *The Day You Begin*. Her goal was to design engaging activities that would be enjoyable. She hoped that the activities would enable her students to continue supportive conversations with each other. In generating the list of possible activities, she made a point to provide options that were aligned with the preferred learning styles of the children in her classroom.

Sofia's Follow-Up Activities

- Go on a scavenger hunt in search of ways that you are like other kids in this class. Be sure to chat with everyone in your class and your teacher. Write down their names and what you have in common. Design a poster that explains what you discovered in your scavenger hunt. Share the poster with your new friends.

- Interview your classmates about their favorite foods that they might want to share with their new classmates. With what you have learned from them, create a menu of "Our Favorite Foods for Lunch" to display in the classroom and help Ms. Sofia plan a special class picnic lunch.
- Write a note to a new student in your classroom who shares something in common with you. Describe why you are happy that you have discovered this. Write the note on fancy paper, seal it in an envelope, and deliver it to your new friend.
- Draw a picture that represents all of the kids in your classroom and how each student is unique. Draw another picture that represents how all the students are alike in some way.
- Write the lyrics to a song that celebrates how happy you are to be a part of Ms. Sofia's second-grade class.
- Create a cheer for the kids in your classroom to begin the start of each and every day. The cheer should remind us how we are unique but also alike in many ways.
- Using the materials in Ms. Sofia's art center, create a sculpture that represents all of the children in your classroom.
- Write a letter to Jacqueline Woodson, the author of *The Day You Begin*, about what you have learned from this story. Explain how her story helped you to understand some important lessons.
- In your private journal, write a message to Angelina about what you learned from her. Tell her how you feel about what you learned.

Sofia's Reflections

Sofia Morales was pleased with what she had developed for her first lesson and was energized by this work. She reflected on other picture books that she had in her collection at home and decided that she would extend her guidance efforts with a second book that she would use with her students later in the first week of school. Sofia wanted to expand upon the message delivered by Jacqueline Woodson in *The Day You Begin* to ensure that children from low-income backgrounds felt welcome in her classroom. She knew just which book she would incorporate and went to her picture book collection to find her copy of Mary Whitcomb's (1998) *Odd Velvet*, one of Sofia's favorite "classics" for second graders.

Odd Velvet

In Mary Whitcomb's story, Velvet is a new student in school who doesn't exactly fit in, but she succeeds in showing her new classmates just how empowering it can be to simply be yourself. Sofia believed that Velvet's poignant story was one that many children from low-income backgrounds would identify with. In the story, Velvet's classmates arrive on the first day of school with gifts of cinnamon tea, lace handkerchiefs, and heart-shaped boxes of potpourri for their teacher. Velvet is excited to give her new teacher an egg carton box filled with seven rocks, her favorite red shoelaces, and half a sparrow's egg. Her classmates are stunned. When the students discover that the lunch in Velvet's brown paper bag is just a butter sandwich and carrots and her dress on the first day of school is not new, the children decide that Velvet is odd. Velvet proudly shares a milkweed pod for show and tell, she wears a sweater that used to belong to her older sister, and she has a pack of only eight crayons! No one wants to be different like Velvet and although the children are polite to her, they certainly do not choose her for partner play or walk home with her after school. When Velvet wins a school art contest using only eight crayons, her classmates marvel at her talent and their attitudes begin to change. The teacher invites Velvet to speak to the class about her rock collection and the children start to appreciate her. But on the day Velvet hands out her handmade invitations to her birthday party, the students remain uneasy because they are not sure they want to attend the party at Velvet's home. When the children arrive for the party, there are no birthday magicians or clowns. Instead, the children are invited to turn Velvet's bedroom into a castle. Velvet and her sister show the children how to use their talents and create a delightful birthday celebration using simple materials. On the final day of school, Velvet's classmates bring their teacher flowers, homemade cards, and an impressive collection of rocks. They have decided that even though Velvet is different, maybe she isn't so odd after all.

Sofia's Plan for the Second Session

Overarching themes:

- Being your authentic self
- Creativity can be developed with simple materials

Discussion questions:

- What do you think of Velvet? What do you like about her?
- What was difficult for Velvet being the new student in school? Have you ever been in the same situation? What did you do? What advice would you give to other kids about being the "new kid"?
- Was Velvet really "different" or "odd"? Explain your thinking.
- Why did other children think that Velvet was "different" or "odd"? Were they fair to think this way about her? Why? Why not?
- Have you ever seen other kids in your school have a strong opinion about a new student? What did they do? How did you respond?
- What do you think was special about Velvet? Would you want to be her friend? Why? Why not?
- What was the special story behind Velvet's name? What do we learn about her from that story? Is there a story about how your family chose your name? Tell us that story.
- What helped the children in Velvet's class eventually understand and appreciate who she was? How can we do the same with new students in our classroom? What would you suggest that we do?
- What do you think allowed Velvet to feel so good about who she was? How can we all learn from her?
- What was special about Velvet's birthday party? Why do you think the children enjoyed it so much?
- How does Velvet help to change the way her classmates think? What have the children learned from having Velvet as a new classmate and friend? How can we apply this lesson in our classroom?

Sofia's Follow-Up Activities

- Using just a few crayons, design a poster for your classroom that reminds us of the important lessons we have learned from Velvet.
- Write a long list of all the natural and interesting items that we might be able to bring to school for show and tell. Collect them and bring them to our classroom to share.
- Write a story about the day you were born and how your family chose your name.
- Write the lyrics to a song celebrating Velvet's gifts and talents.

- Design a celebration for your classmates using only simple materials. What will the invitation be? What games and activities will you play?
- In your private journal, write a message to Velvet about what you learned from her. Tell her how you feel about what you learned.

Sofia Morales was pleased with the two lessons she designed for creating a supportive classroom environment for her second graders. She looked forward to presenting the picture books to her students and working to support the emotional well-being of her diverse students. With this work completed, she began to think about how she would tackle those bulletin boards that were waiting for her!

Jenna Explores Perfectionism with Students

3

Jenna Wade was enjoying her fifth year of teaching in the gifted and talented education program in the Arcadia Meadows School District. Jenna often shared with her family and friends that she believed she had an ideal professional situation. She explained that she was intellectually challenged each day, she worked with great teachers, her administrators were supportive of her work, but most importantly, her students were very intelligent kids who kept her energized and laughing every day.

Jenna had transferred to Arcadia Meadows from a neighboring school district where she taught fourth graders in a self-contained classroom. During her early years of teaching, she found that she was discouraged by her inability to adequately address the diverse needs of all of her students, particularly the most capable. Her frustrations eventually led her to earn a master's degree in gifted education from the state university. She excelled in her graduate studies and was thrilled when she had the opportunity to join the gifted education team in Arcadia Meadows. Jenna's itinerant schedule involved teaching in both the elementary and middle school and she especially enjoyed the opportunity to work with the same students from grades two through eight. As a result, she established lasting relationships with her students and their families.

After being in this setting for several years, Jenna observed a trend emerging in the most capable students in the district. She noticed particular behaviors and characteristics in her students that worried her. She reflected on her graduate school coursework and thought back to important class discussions on perfectionism in highly able students. Jenna realized that the perfectionistic characteristics, traits, and behaviors emerging in both her

DOI: 10.4324/9781003235408-3

elementary and middle school students were consistent with what had been highlighted by her professor and described in course readings. She saw a number of the students seemed constantly anxious about making errors in classroom activities. Comments were made by students that reflected their frustration with meeting self-expectations. It was now October and Jenna had learned that Jasmine and Alexis had just dropped out of an after-school dance group because, they explained, "the routines were just too hard." A third-grade teacher had shared that Steven had a meltdown over mistakes he made on a math test. She reflected on another conversation she had recently with Mrs. Ramirez while shopping at the local grocery store. The mother of an eighth-grade athlete, she was concerned about her son Pablo who could not tolerate even mild critique by his soccer coach, and this resulted in tension at home after practice.

One of Jenna's greatest joys in teaching in the gifted program was the opportunity to facilitate the independent research projects that students self-selected. She noticed students who were highly motivated to pursue a project in the past had been rather slow in generating ideas for research this year. She wondered if this was procrastination or were they worried about having to produce what they saw would have to be another outstanding project. As she reflected on her oldest middle school students, she wondered whether these behaviors would continue. She made a note to herself to check in with her colleagues at the high school who taught honors and advanced placement classes. Jenna wanted to ask them if they were observing similar trends in the older gifted students.

As she reflected on this problem, Jenna decided that she would design an intervention within the gifted education program at Arcadia Meadows. She believed that the classroom environment she had worked to establish would enable her students to remain comfortable with her and their peers and honestly discuss the behaviors that concerned her. She would infuse a number of book discussions to focus on perfectionism. With her experience teaching gifted students, Jenna understood that her classroom was perhaps the most appropriate place to hold these conversations about a sensitive issue. She knew that both the elementary and middle school groups would feel more at ease discussing perfectionism with their gifted and talented peers rather than in a larger discussion in their regular classrooms. Jenna understood the complexity of the issue and would plan her lessons accordingly.

The Girl Who Never Made Mistakes

Jenna turned to her classroom collection of books and decided to introduce one of her favorite picture books that addressed this issue. She would begin with *The Girl Who Never Made Mistakes* by Mark Pett and Gary Rubinstein (2011) in which the protagonist Beatrice Bottomwell is known for being perfect. She never forgets her math homework, she always matches her socks, and she always wins the annual school talent show. Beatrice is known throughout her town as "The Girl Who Never Makes Mistakes" until one day, the inevitable occurs. Beatrice makes a huge mistake in front of the entire community and discovers that it's really healthy to be able to enjoy daily adventures and laugh at our mistakes along the way.

Jenna's Lesson

Overarching themes:

- Learning to laugh at our mistakes
- Maintaining healthy self-expectations

Discussion questions:

- How was Beatrice Bottomwell different from her younger brother Carl? How are you different from your siblings? What do you enjoy about them?
- Why do you think Beatrice used exactly the same amount of peanut butter as jelly when she made a sandwich for her brother's lunch? What does this say about her?
- Why do you think Beatrice Bottomwell was a celebrity in her town? How might this have affected her? Do you know of kids who face similar pressures? What have you noticed about how they handle their situation?
- When Beatrice was on a cooking team with her two best friends Millie and Sarah, she came really close to making a mistake. How did she respond to this experience? What do you think of her behavior?
- After her "almost mistake," how did Beatrice change? Why do you think of the changes in her? What advice would you want to give her?

- What happened that caused Beatrice to make a mistake at the talent show? How did she respond to her huge mistake? What do you think of her reaction? If you were in Beatrice's situation, how do you think you would have responded? Why?
- How did the audience support Beatrice after she made her big mistake? Has anyone ever helped you after you've made a mistake? What did they do? How did they help you?
- Why do you think Beatrice slept so well after her big mistake at the talent show? What can we learn from this?
- Why do you think Beatrice began to wear socks that didn't match? How might that help her?
- Beatrice and her brother started enjoying lunches that were messy and delicious by eating Inside Out PB & J! How might that help Beatrice and Carl?
- Beatrice joined Millie and Sarah skating in the park and joined them in skating and falling a lot. How might that help Beatrice and her friends?
- People stopped calling Beatrice "The Girl Who Never Makes Mistakes." How do you think she felt about that? If you were given a nickname like that, how might you respond?
- Was Beatrice more fun to be with after she made her big mistake? Would you want to be her friend? Explain why.

Follow-Up Activities

- After Beatrice made her big mistake, she learned to have fun in different ways. Help Beatrice by creating a list of many more ways she could make mistakes on purpose for fun. When you have written your list of suggestions, send them to Beatrice in an e-mail message!
- Design a poster that celebrates the biggest mistake you've ever made and how you learned to laugh about it.
- Write the lyrics for a song that Beatrice will enjoy singing about having made a big mistake.
- Design posters for your classroom that help kids understand why it's important to learn from their mistakes.
- Plan a party to celebrate the lessons you've learned from Beatrice. Design a messy and delicious lunch menu for the party. Design a fun dance to enjoy. Design a fun game to play.

Be a Perfect Person in Just Three Days!

After designing the picture book lesson, Jenna decided to consider extending her instruction with one of her favorite chapter books on the topic of perfectionism. She knew that her older elementary students would appreciate *Be a Perfect Person in Just Three Days!* by Stephen Manes (2018). Jenna viewed Manes' work as a classic and believed the message the author delivered remained contemporary. Stephen Manes introduced his readers to Milo Crinkley, a boy who discovers a book in his school library that really piques his interest. The title *Be a Perfect Person in Just Three Days!* sounds interesting and even though Milo thinks the author Dr. K. Pinkerton Silverfish looks somewhat weird, he claims to be the world's leading authority on perfection. Milo takes the book home and follows its instructions. Dr. Silverfish directs his readers to hang a stalk of broccoli from their necks for one day, spend another day without consuming food, and spend a third day doing nothing!

Jenna's Second Lesson

Overarching themes:

- Being perfect is impossible
- Learning to laugh at our mistakes
- Enjoying one's imperfections
- Maintaining healthy self-expectations

Discussion questions:

- What did Milo Crinkley do that made him feel he wasn't perfect?
- Why did Milo think it would be great to be perfect? What do you think of how he saw the situations in which he made mistakes? Do you ever have experiences like Milo's? How do you respond to your mistakes?
- Milo spent a day hanging a stalk of broccoli from his neck. Why do you think he was able to go along with this first part of Dr. Silverfish's plan in becoming a perfect person?
- How did Milo survive his day wearing the stalk of broccoli? What do you think enabled him to do this? What do you believe he learned from this experience?

- When Milo returned home from a day of school wearing the stalk of broccoli around his neck, how did he behave? Why do you think he responded to the day's events that way? What does that tell us about Milo? Would you have done the same?
- As part of Dr. Silverfish's plan, Milo went an entire day without eating. What do you think this says about his willpower? How do you think you might have responded to this part of the plan? Describe what you think might have happened to you.
- In Dr. Silverfish's plan for perfection, he asked Milo to spend 24 hours doing nothing. What did this assignment do to Milo? How do you think you would have responded to this? Describe what you think might have happened to you.
- Why do you think Milo's father was supportive of Milo following the three steps of Dr. Silverfish's plan toward perfection?
- What was the most important lesson that Milo learned from reading Dr. Silverfish's book?
- Dr. Silverfish concludes his book with an important message for his readers. He says:

> You know what perfect is? Perfect is not eating or drinking or talking or moving a muscle or even making the teeniest mistake. Perfect is never doing anything wrong – which means never doing anything at all. Perfect is boring!
>
> (p. 29)

What do you think of this message?
- At the end of the story, the author described Milo's performance in a baseball game:

> He dropped a fly ball for a triple, he let a grounder skip through his legs for a home run, and he struck out with the bases loaded. His teammates got angry with him, and even the manager looked annoyed...Normally, Milo would have been upset with himself. But today he was calm. "Nobody's perfect," he said with a shrug. And he went out and made a brilliant catch of a long fly ball. It wasn't enough to save the game for his team, but it felt good.
>
> (p. 31)

What do we learn from that passage? What do you think the author wants us to understand?

- What's the most important idea you gained from reading and discussing this book? How can you apply it to your life in and out of school?

Jenna's Follow-Up Activities

- Write and role play a conversation between Beatrice Bottomwell and Milo Crinkley about never making mistakes.
- Design a recipe for becoming more relaxed in life. What will you include for ingredients? How will you prepare this delicious treat?
- Design posters for your classroom that deliver important messages about self-care.
- Design posters for your classroom that celebrate taking a risk.
- Design posters for your classroom that celebrate having fun versus winning and being the "best."
- Using the art supplies available, create a sculpture that represents the imperfections that make us more interesting.
- Design coupons for your classmates to be redeemed for being messy, late, incomplete, or imperfect for a day.
- Write yourself a permission slip to make at least three mistakes today. Smile when they happen.
- In your reflective journal, respond to one of the following prompts:
    What makes being perfect seem so important?
    Perfectionism is often quiet and hidden.

A YA Novel for Jenna's Eighth Graders: *We Regret to Inform You*

Having watched her students move on to Arcadia Meadows High School, Jenna planned to have helpful conversations with the Honors and AP teachers to check in on what they were seeing with the gifted students. She remained concerned that the perfectionistic tendencies evident in her younger students would continue. She decided that with her eighth graders she would extend her book discussions to include a young adult novel. She thought her eighth graders would appreciate a book that examined high-achieving students and their experience dealing with the pressures of college admission.

She decided on Ariel Kaplan's (2018) *We Regret to Inform You.* In this novel, Mischa, a senior at Blanchard High School, is the model student behind the perfectly well-rounded college application. When she is rejected by Ivy League universities and her safety school, she is devastated. All of the sacrifices her single mother made to send her to prep school, the long nights cramming for exams, and the résumé-boosting extracurricular activities amount to nothing. When she discovers her transcript was hacked, she connects with a group of high school techies to launch an investigation that rocks the quiet community of Blanchard Prep to its stately foundations. Through Mischa's experience, Blanchard students are reminded that they are more than their test scores and GPA.

Jenna's Lesson for Her Eighth Graders

- What do you think of Mischa? Some may describe her as an overachiever. Would you agree? Why? Why not? Is there such a thing as overachieving?
- Do students who are conscientious get labeled as overachievers? What is the difference between being conscientious and being perfectionistic? Explain some examples.
- Do the stress and peer pressure to be on top portrayed in this novel seem realistic to you? Have you seen this in your older siblings in high school?
- Early in the novel, Mischa describes what she is experiencing in school:

> I hadn't gotten any emails yet, but I knew other people were hearing as responses trickled in and people would let out stifled little shrieks in the middle of class. After calculus, I saw girls standing puffy-eyed in the bathroom, staring unmoving at their own reflections, and I wondered who had turned them down.
>
> (p. 15)

- What does this tell us about the culture of her high school? Would you anticipate this happening with your friends when you're in high school? Why? How will you want to handle this? How might you begin to think about your plans for what you would like to do after high school?

- Mischa visited Georgetown University as a young child, and she described the students on campus: "I'd never seen so many people who looked so happy in one place. And why shouldn't they be happy? Shining stars, every one of them, passing through on their way to a bigger, better life" (p. 25).

  What does this tell us about her views of the future? What does it say about her?

- Describe the sacrifices that Mischa's mother has made to send her daughter to Blanchard Prep. What would you say to other parents of highly capable students about planning for their futures?

- Is having high aspirations healthy? Explain.

- In reading Mischa's story, we learn important lessons about having fun and not taking life too seriously. How might we apply those lessons in our lives?

- When Mischa learns that she has not been admitted to any of the colleges she applied to, she describes her response saying," I felt a little like I was swimming through Jell-O" (p. 30). What do you think she means? Have you ever had an experience where you felt that way? What did you do?

- Some high school kids get heavily involved in school clubs and activities. Mischa described her thinking about her role in student government saying:

  > I'm the vice-president, a position I chose strategically because it involves less work than any of the other three main positions (I don't have to deal with money, keep the minutes, or delegate to other people), which frees me up for more activities than I could have managed otherwise.
  >
  > (p. 30)

- Why would Mischa think this way? What does this tell us about the pressure that high highly capable high school students face? How do you think teenagers should handle such pressure?

- At one point, Mischa begins to doubt her abilities:

  > I was just another person, another salmon trying to make it upstream, and the current had been too much for me. The magnitude of my failure pulled me down, down, down, until I felt like I was at the bottom of the ocean, looking up at

everyone around me through ten million gallons of water. I would never be able to make this up to Mom. Never.

(p. 42)

Do you think that Mischa's mother placed too much pressure on her daughter? Do you think Mischa's pressure was self-inflicted? Explain.

- How would you describe the level of competition in Mischa's high school? How has the school culture shaped the experiences of Mischa, Meredith, Nate, and Caroline? How have they responded to it differently?
- How did the culture of competition at Blanchard Prep affect friendships?
- Nate eventually opens up to Mischa about his burnout experience in eighth grade and his placement at Meadow House for psychiatric care. Why do you think he shares that information with her? How does she respond? How does her new knowledge of Nate's past help her?
- Mischa notices that students are responding to the news of her college admission situation strangely. She says:

> I suddenly understood the way everyone was looking at me. It wasn't just pity; it was also fear. And it's not like I didn't understand why I was scary. I was a reminder of how precarious everything was for all of us. Our lives were like a very neatly ordered stack of dominos, precisely lined up.
>
> (p. 131)

- Would you say this statement by Mischa is accurate? Do you think that teenagers who struggle with perfectionism think this way? Explain.
- Mischa says to Nate:

> I used to get up every morning knowing exactly who I was and what I had to do...I went after every brass ring someone put in front of me. I was really, really good at that. And now that's over. I have no idea who I am now.
>
> (p. 166)

- Do you think that teenagers shape their identity by measuring their achievements?
- Of all of the characters you met in the novel, which would you say you learned from the most? How did that character's experience shape your thinking?

- What important lessons from *We Regret to Inform You* do you hope to apply to your life as you begin high school?

Follow-Up Activities

- Nate had a mascot named "Maury" at home that helped him keep his life in perspective. Design a mascot for Ms. Wade's gifted education classroom that will remind students of the need to maintain a healthy balance between school and having fun. Give students the opportunity to vote on a name for the mascot and have fun creating costumes for the mascot.
- Many readers might feel strongly that Mishca should have been the student to deliver the commencement speech. Write the speech for her. What message does she want to leave Blanchard Prep as her legacy?
- You have been given the opportunity to write a letter of recommendation for Mishca's college applications. How will your letter read?
- Design posters for Ms. Wade's gifted education classroom that remind students of the need to maintain healthy self-expectations.
- In your journal, respond to one of the following prompts:

    Provide Mishca with your personal advice for negotiating her life following her gap year.

    Explain any lessons you learned about yourself from reading and reflecting on this novel.

Jenna Wade Continues Her Work

Having reflected on the important messages delivered by Ariel Kaplan in *We Regret to Inform You*, Jenna decided to extend her work with the eighth graders further. She thought back to several of her former students who were currently enrolled at Arcadia Meadows High who she believed would be great effective speakers to invite to her classroom to have conversations with her eighth graders. She knew that middle school students would listen closely to cool teenagers who were presently experiencing the pressures that intelligent high-achieving students faced in high school. She believed that an hour's conversation with them could influence her students in many positive ways.

Luke Examines Identity Development with Teenagers

Luke Henderson ended his day of classes at Wildewood High School with his honors American literature students. In early November, he stood at the back of his classroom surveying his group. He was relieved that the school's homecoming festivities were over, and he was able to get his students focused on academics again before they left for the holidays. As his students were engaged in reading his assigned literary selections, he enjoyed a few quiet moments from the back of his classroom and reflected on the gifted teenagers in his class.

Luke noticed that Pablo looked exhausted again this week and wondered just how many hours he was working at the local grocery store. He paused and wrote a note to himself to explore that issue with him. He knew that Pablo's father was recently laid off from his work and wondered if Pablo was taking on the role of "man of the house." He smiled to himself as he took note of Andrew's rather outlandish new hairstyle, perhaps an indication that another chapter of adolescent rebellion was about to begin. He watched as Ebony read from her iPad and wrote reflective notes in her calligraphy-like penmanship. Ebony seemed to enjoy his class yet Luke worried that her conscientious work habits were bordering on perfection-ism. She had shared with her teacher earlier in the year that her goal was to graduate as class valedictorian and Luke wondered if that was how she measured her self-image.

Luke noted that Josh appeared to be rather calm considering the major milestone in his adolescent life that had occurred over the weekend. Josh had come out to his friends on Instagram and his peers had responded by posting supportive comments. Luke hoped that as a gay teenager, Josh would continue to benefit from the support of his friends as long as he was enrolled at Wildewood. As Luke Henderson walked to the front of his

DOI: 10.4324/9781003235408-4

classroom, he stopped at Seth's desk and gently nudged him to wake him from another nap. He was frustrated with Seth and wanted to let him know how he felt about this student with so much potential, the self-proclaimed "Slacker King of Wildewood High." Just as he aroused Seth, the school's intercom came alive, and the end of the day announcements concluded the seventh period class. As his students began to leave, Luke reminded them of the essay assignment he would be collecting the following day and wished them a pleasant evening.

He was happy that his afternoon schedule did not include another school committee meeting as he packed his bag to leave for the day. He was meeting Olivia Landers at a nearby coffee shop and was looking forward to seeing his friend and commiserating with another English teacher. He and Olivia had graduated from the university together, and Olivia was currently teaching at the local middle school. As he waited for his friend to arrive at the downtown coffee shop, he reread an article from an education journal. As he read the article describing how teachers can address the psychosocial needs of teenagers through high-quality literature, Luke became intrigued with the author's rationale for using such an approach with gifted students.

Olivia Landers arrived just as Luke finished reading the article. While Luke waited for his friend to purchase her cup of coffee, he reflected on his students in his honors American literature class, the challenges they faced in adolescence, and the variety of ways their identities were taking shape. The article had him thinking about how he would approach an important instructional unit in his course. Because he and Olivia had always enjoyed exchanging ideas about teaching strategies, he was eager to share his thinking about the article and how he night infuse several young adult novels into his curriculum in order to address some of the identity development issues facing his students. As Olivia approached the table, Luke announced with a big smile, "Hi! I'm so glad you're here! I can't wait to share a new idea with you."

When Olivia returned to the table with her cup of coffee, they checked in with each other regarding their families and the news of the day at both the middle and high school. After catching up, Olivia asked, "So tell me, what's this new idea that you're so excited about?" Luke shared the educational article he had read and described how he was thinking of incorporating several contemporary young adult novels in his next unit in his honors course. He explained the overarching theme he wanted to address was identity. Olivia smiled as she explained that her middle school students reminded her of this issue as she described the daily "emotional roller coaster ride" her seventh and eighth graders experienced as young adolescents. In return, Luke described what he had recently observed in his students, from Ebony's image of herself as valedictorian to Seth's identity as a "slacker" and Josh's newly revealed identity as a gay male.

Olivia agreed with Luke that infusing several contemporary novels with those suggested by the school district's curriculum guide would be beneficial to students. She reached for a notepad and pen from her bag and began jotting down titles of young adult novels that she wanted Luke to investigate. Luke reached for his laptop and started searching the internet for novels that examined identity development. An hour quickly passed, and the two dedicated teachers realized they needed to head home to their families; however, they were both energized about Luke's plans. Olivia promised to continue searching for more novels for Luke to consider and she promised him that she would explore how she might incorporate the same approach with her gifted middle school students. Olivia commented, "After all, you really cannot begin too early in helping these kids with their identity drama!"

Following an exhaustive search, Luke enjoyed reading a variety of young adult novels and narrowed down his choices. He decided he would provide two options for his students. He chose *American Panda* by Gloria Chao (2018) and *Deacon Locke Went to Prom* by Brian Katcher (2017). Not only did he enjoy reading the two novels, but he also had fun generating the discussion questions he would use to facilitate the conversation with his students and a variety of follow-up activities he would offer the class.

American Panda

Luke planned to have his students engage in a classic novel in American literature that examined identity development in adolescence. He thought back to his high school English classes and remembered several of his favorites that explored identity development: Chaim Potok's (1987) *The Chosen* and Robert Pirsig's (2006). *Zen and the Art of Motorcycle Maintenance*. He thought he might want to select a more recent novel so he reviewed the curriculum guide provided by his district and thought Gary Paulsen's (2014) *The Island* might be an appropriate choice. In this novel, Paulsen delivers the story of a young man who needs personal space throughout his adolescence as he struggles to find his identity. Luke was eager to have his students compare and contrast the work of Paulsen with the two more contemporary selections he had discovered. He wondered whether or not his students would identify with the protagonists in each novel and learn important lessons that they might apply to their own lives. Moreover, would they find it easy enough to compare and contrast the novels to Paulsen's work and find similarities that might reinforce the important messages about identity formation?

Following a week of instruction on Gary Paulsen's novel, he was pleased to see just how much his students enjoyed the work. He then shifted to the exploration of *American Panda*. In this novel, the protagonist, Mei Lu, is a 17-year-old freshman at MIT who is on track to fulfill the pre-determined future her parents have established. She is to become a doctor, marry a preapproved Taiwanese Ivy Leaguer, and provide her parents with many grandchildren. With everything that her parents have given up making life comfortable for her, she cannot disappoint her family. Under the weight of the expectations of her parents, she begins to unravel as she struggles with the truth about herself: she is a germophobe who cannot stomach the thought of attending medical school, she falls asleep in biology lectures, and she is developing a strong crush on Darren Takahashi, a Japanese American classmate. When she connects with her older brother who is estranged from her family for dating the wrong woman, Mei begins to question if all her secrets are truly worth it. Mei has to find a way to be herself.

Luke's Plan for the Session

Overarching themes:

- Balancing family expectations against one's own secret ambitions
- Complex familial relationships
- Understanding cultural stereotypes

Discussion questions:

- What do you enjoy most about Mei Lu? What would you say are her most positive characteristics? Is she someone you might enjoy having as a friend? Why? Why not?

- Mei Lu is accelerated in her schooling. How do you think her early entrance into college influences how she views herself?
- Early in the novel we meet Mrs. Lu and Mei describes a conversation with her mother:

> "Actually, I have this friend – remember Mrs. Huang? Her son is interested in meeting you. Eugene is Taiwanese, a senior at Harvard, and will be a good husband. He's applying to medical schools now" She began pawing at my blunt bangs as if she were Edward Scissorhands. "We'll have to clean up this mess before you meet him. Really, Mei, why do you insist on having these? Just to give me a heart attack?"
>
> (p. 9)

What does this say about Mei's relationship with her mother? How does this scenario help us to understand the parental expectations that Mei faces?

- Later in the novel, Mei describes her taking notice of Darren Takahashi. What does the following description of this encounter say about her? How important is it that we appreciate this passage to understand how she views herself?

> At orientation, his head had bobbed above the sea of freshmen, and I had been attracted to his spiky anime hair. It had taken me half an hour to work up the courage to smile at him, but he'd been too busy laughing with the perky blonde beside him to notice shy, not-blonde me. My heart had lurched, and then I had traveled back in time to first grade. Wooden desk. Chalkboard overhead. And six-year-old me looking from one classmate to another, wishing I didn't look so different.
>
> (p. 11)

- How complex is Mei's relationship with her parents? Have you known of teenagers who faced similar situations? What did they do to cope with parental expectations?
- Mei describes a scenario in which she and her parents are dining together in a local restaurant and her father makes a critical family announcement:

As I was about to dig in, my father cleared his throat – a thundering noise that always made me sit up straight and lower my eyes. "Mei, a few words." He paused for effect. "MIT is your first step to a good life. Work hard, get good grades, get into a good medical school, and make us proud. Don't worry, we will be watching every step of the way. We will see you here at Chow, Chow every Saturday, to check in." A decree, not a request...I wanted to enjoy my newfound freedom and cut the umbilical cord, but with these words I realized it would never be severed, only stretched.

(p. 16)

If you could have a conversation with Mei following this visit with her parents, what would you say to her? What advice would you provide her? How important is it for gifted students to "cut or stretch the umbilical cord" in order to shape their own identity?

- Mei has several experiences as a freshman at MIT that begin to help her in understanding who she is becoming. Which events at the beginning of her academic year have an impact on how she sees herself? Why are these experiences important to her? What do you learn through Mei's experiences that might help to prepare you for your first year in college?

- Mei describes a significant experience in the following passage:

I kicked off my shoes, one flick of the ankle, then another, and the second my socks met the floor, my movements morphed. I was always a dancer – that was a part of me, not something that could be separated – and alone in this vast space, I stopped holding back.

My pointed feet slid across the linoleum as if they were intimately acquainted. My curved, extended arms swept through the air, and I leaped, spun, and *pas-de-chat*-ed my way to the other side of the room. I had found my space...It was worth having to disinfect these socks now...Even though I was exerting myself, my breathing was easier here. Natural. It was the one place where I could express myself, be completely me. If only I could find another who spoke dance.

(p. 24)

What do we learn about Mei through this scenario? How do you feel about her after reading this? What would you want to say to her?

- How do our gifts and talents shape who we become as individuals? How strong are they in influencing the formation of identity?
- Mei is aware of the sacrifices her parents have made for their children. She explains:

> I've always been jealous of my friends whose parents kissed their cheeks, read them bedtime stories, bought them whatever toys they wanted. But my parents showed love in different ways: shopping exclusively at garage sales, reusing napkins and Ziplocs, never treating themselves to the furniture or vacations they coveted. It was so I could go to the best school and end up with a stable career where I would never have to sacrifice like they did. To them, a secure future was the ultimate gift a parent could give. How could I refuse them this when this was their motivation?
>
> (p. 80)

Do you know of similar situations among teenagers in your high school? What have you learned from them? How might teachers and school counselors support them?

- How does Mei's relationship with Darren influence her identity as a gifted young woman? Why is their friendship so significant?
- How does Mei's relationship with her brother influence who she becomes? How do they support each other as brother and sister? How can sibling relationships shape who we become as individuals?
- How was Mei Lu resilient? How do you think this resilience supported her as a college student? Have there been times in your life when you needed to develop resilience to overcome adversity? How did that evolve?
- How does Mei reconcile her relationship with her parents? Do you believe she approached this difficult situation appropriately? Why? Why not? What advice do you think she would give other teenagers?

After preparing his discussion questions, Luke moved on to generate several enjoyable follow-up activities for students to engage in following their reading of the novel. Luke recognized that a number of his students might closely identify with Mei Lu's challenges with parental expectations and would need some quiet time for introspection. With that in mind, he made sure to provide options that students would handle privately. Luke assumed that they might appreciate the opportunity to reflect on the author's message through private journaling, therefore, he provided a menu of journal prompts. He also planned to provide students the option of working collaboratively on the follow-up activity they chose.

Luke's Follow-Up Activities

- Design an artistic representation of Mei Lu's story and the significant lessons learned from her.
- Create a mobile to hang from the ceiling of the classroom that captures the essential lessons about identity that you have learned from Mei Lu's story.
- Construct a silhouette of yourself and artistically represent the various components of your identity within the silhouette.
- Using the free digital tools available online, design a "word cloud" to represent your identity. Present yourself creatively and include hobbies, values, goals in school and life in general, and something interesting about you.
- Write a poem describing the identity formation experiences of gifted teenagers.
- Write song lyrics to describe Mei Lu's experiences in *American Panda*.
- Mei Lu visits Wildewood High School as a guest speaker for the graduating senior class. Write her speech.
- Reflect on one of the following prompts in your journal:
  - What was most inspirational in Mei Lu's life story? How might this novel influence you?
  - Craft an e-mail message to Mei Lu seeking her advice about growing up as a culturally diverse gifted student. How will your message read? Write her response.
  - Write a letter to Mei Lu's parents in which you share your thoughts on how their daughter's many talents need nurturing.

Deacon Locke Went to Prom

Luke was delighted with his students' response to *American Panda* and was eager to continue his instructional unit with the study of *Deacon Locke Went to Prom*. In this novel, Deacon Locke is an awkward high school senior who does not think he can get a date for the prom and decides to take his best friend, his grandmother, as his date. He gets ready for the prom by taking dance lessons from Soraya, a gorgeous girl unlike any other he has ever met. He stumbles into accidental fame when a video of him and his prom date goes viral. From then on, Deacon's life with his grandmother, Soraya, and his high school peers becomes more complex than he ever could have imagined.

Luke's Plan for the Session

Overarching themes:

- Identity development
- Loyalty in friendship
- The role of social media in adolescent life
- Challenging xenophobia

Discussion questions:

- Why do you think that Deacon hesitates to ask Kelli to the prom? Have you had friends who faced a similar situation? What advice did you give them? How did they respond?
- What do you think of the relationship between Deacon and his grandmother? What do you think is special about Jean and how she nurtures her grandson?
- What is the significance of promposals at Fayetteville High School? What does this say about how teenagers view themselves? How might this influence friendships?
- Why is the astronomy hill so important to Deacon? Do you have a similar space in your life that supports you? If so, what does that quiet space do for you?

- Kelli says to Deacon, "I know there's an interesting guy in that big blockhead of yours, somewhere. Maybe. Try to let him out sometimes." (p. 50). What is she saying to Deacon? What do think of Kelli's advice for Deacon?
- Soraya explains to Deacon:

> That's why I started dancing. I guess every little girl around here takes a dance class at some point in her life. I just wanted to fit in. I mean, my mother was the only woman in my neighborhood who wore a hijab. Dancing made me feel more like everyone else. And, by the time I got to junior high, I realized I kind of liked it.
>
> (p. 69)

- What does this say about Soraya's cultural identity? How might the development of identity be different for culturally diverse students in our school?
- Share your thoughts about the following passage from the novel in which Deacon says:

> Wow. We did it. We're here at the dance. *I'm* here at the dance. Deacon Locke, the guy who once hid in the bathroom on the day we had to give oral reports in eighth grade. I made it to prom. It's a pretty good feeling.
>
> (p. 95)

Can you think of a moment in your life that was similar? Describe that for us.

- As the prom concludes, Soraya shares her thoughts about Deacon and his courage in taking his grandmother to the prom. What is her message to him? What do you think of her understanding of Deacon?
- The morning after the prom, Elijah announces to Deacon, "I didn't film it! But look, over two thousand hits since last night. You've gone viral!" How does this event influence the remainder of Deacon's life in high school? How might instant notoriety influence how a young man like Deacon conducts himself? What are the challenges that teenagers face when they encounter overnight fame?

- Deacon struggles to accept the invitation to become part of *Celebrity Dance Off*. What do you think his greatest concerns are? Why? If you were in his situation, what would you do?
- Deacon gets into a serious fight over racist comments directed at Soraya. What does this tell us about his identity development?
- When Deacon struggles with his decision to be a contestant on *Celebrity Dance Off*, Soraya insists that he take advantage of the opportunity. She says:

> Because you're not that great of a dancer. You're good, but not great. The reason you've been invited to this thing is because people like you. You're sweet and nice and funny when you let yourself be. I know it. Jean knows it. Those TV people know it. And they want to pay you and make you famous, at least for a while. I'm not going to be the girl who sits here and tells you to give all that up.
>
> (p. 165)

What does her message to Deacon say about how he presents himself?
- Mr. Delaney, the TV agent with *Celebrity Dance Off* becomes concerned when Deacon ends up in a fight. He explains, "We work hard to maintain the image of our dancers. You were supposed to be this year's yokel." He continues, "Oh, you know...the country boy. The hillbilly trying to find his way around the big city. The audience loves that" (p. 179).

  If you were in Deacon's situation, how might you respond to this comment?
- Throughout the novel, Deacon does everything he can to protect his grandmother's well-being. Describe what he does for her that highlights how his identity as a gifted young man is taking shape.
- What characteristics, personality traits, and behaviors do you admire most about Deacon Locke? Why?
- If you were to write the sequel to this young adult novel, what would you want to happen with Deacon and his high school friends?

Luke's Follow-Up Activities

- Social media plays an important role in Deacon Locke's story. If you could post a message to him on Instagram, what would you say? Write that message.
- In this novel, Deacon Locke never wins a dance trophy. Create an artistic representation of the trophy you would want to present to Deacon that represents all that is good about this young man.
- Using your cell phone camera, take five photographs that represent Deacon Locke's identity. Create a photographic collage and include captions to explain your interpretation.
- Using simple art materials, create a sculpture that represents the identity development process experienced by culturally diverse teenagers.
- Imagine that Deacon Locke returns home after competing in *Celebrity Dance Off* and he is invited to speak to middle school students in his community. Write Deacon's speech for that event.
- Write a letter to Deacon's grandmother letting her know what you admire about Deacon.
- Plan a special celebratory dance event for your school in which every student is to accompany a family member as their date. Consider the theme for the event, advertisements, the decorations, and the music selection.
- Design a *Celebrity Dance Off* experience for your school in which students must perform a dance that best represents their personal identity. Have friends demonstrate their dances in class.

Luke was pleased with his plans for the unit in his honors literature class. He was eager to share his work with Olivia to see if she might have suggestions for improvements. He was even more excited about facilitating the discussion of the two new novels and having his students explore their identity at such an important time in their adolescence. He reflected on how influential this instruction would be for his students and he looked forward to what he thought would be fascinating conversations with them.

Jenna and Susan Collaborate to Support Twice-Exceptional Students

Jenna Wade, the gifted education teacher at Arcadia Meadows Elementary School enjoyed her relationships with supportive colleagues. She discovered early on that the culture of the school encouraged collaboration among teachers and staff. She was also fortunate to have a classroom across the hall from Susan Grisanti, a resource room teacher for students with learning disabilities. Susan was a new teacher at Arcadia Meadows and Jenna found her to be very passionate about her work with children who faced learning challenges. Jenna and Susan spent many afternoons in their classrooms having rich conversations about teaching and studying the learning profiles of students. In doing so, they were successful in identifying a population of twice-exceptional (2e) students in a number of classrooms at Arcadia Meadows. As a result, these children benefitted from services in both Susan's resource room and Jenna's gifted education classroom. From graduate studies in their respective fields, both Jenna and Susan recognized that this special population of children faced challenges in their social and emotional development. They observed these students experiencing stress and frustration that impacted their self-esteem. They recognized challenges with identity development and observed that these children had difficulties with peer relationships. Having identified this population, Jenna and Susan understood there was a need for these students to understand the diagnosis of twice-exceptionality as well and a concomitant need to learn how to live with the disability (Hébert, 2020).

Jenna and Susan agreed that they wanted their students to understand that being a different type of learner was not a deficit. They would insist that the children focus on their gifts and celebrate their strengths. They would have the children understand that 2e individuals often recognize

DOI: 10.4324/9781003235408-5

their intuition as a strength and take great pride in their resilience (Hébert, 2020). Jenna and Susan agreed on implementing a strength-based approach to teaching these children. In addition to facilitating discussions that would guide these students to understanding themselves as twice-exceptional, they would teach stress management as well as share biographies of successful gifted individuals with learning disabilities. Lastly, Jenna and Susan agreed that their work with this group of students would incorporate helping students appreciate their intuitive qualities, celebrate their creativity, and see the value of developing resilience.

Since Jenna had enjoyed her earlier book discussions that focused on perfectionism with gifted students, she was now eager to incorporate this strategy with the group of identified twice-exceptional students. She thought that a collaborative approach to facilitating book discussions with the 2e students would be great. Susan agreed with Jenna. The students would benefit greatly from talking about their experiences with both teachers who were concerned about their well-being. One afternoon after school, Jenna and Susan met and began to plan their lessons. They both enjoyed a love of children's literature and found that it was quite easy to generate a list of possible books that would speak to the issues facing their students. They decided to begin with a classic, *Eggbert: The Slightly Cracked Egg* by Tom Ross (1997).

Eggbert: The Slightly Cracked Egg

The picture book Jenna and Susan selected presents the poignant story of Eggbert, an egg who wears a red beret and carries a palette and brush as he enjoys painting for his friends in the refrigerator. When they discover a crack in Eggbert's shell, he is banished from the fridge. He has to search for a new place to live. In his challenge to find a new home, he discovers that his artistic talents enable him to camouflage himself as he paints himself into the landscape. Eventually, Eggbert notices the sun shining through a crack in the sky and realizes that the world is filled with wonderful cracks. As he accepts his imperfection, he travels around the world to visit famous cracked sights – a canyon, an island volcano, and even the Liberty Bell. Throughout his travels, Eggbert paints postcards of his adventures to send to the eggs back in the refrigerator. From his journey, Eggbert realizes that it is rather wonderful being slightly cracked.

Jenna and Susan's Lesson Plan

Overarching themes:

- Sensitivity and empathy in twice-exceptional students
- Camouflaging one's weaknesses
- Overcoming adversity
- Perseverance
- Being true to self
- Imperfections make people more interesting
- Having a strong belief in self

Discussion questions:

- What did you like about Eggbert?
- Why do you think Eggbert's paintings cheered up the other eggs in the refrigerator? Do you have special talents that your friends enjoy? Describe them.
- What does it mean to be "slightly cracked"? Do you think all people are "slightly cracked"? How might we be "slightly cracked"?
- How do you explain what it means to be twice-exceptional?
- Do you think twice-exceptional kids see themselves as slightly cracked? If so, how?
- Why do you think Eggbert painted himself to blend right in with his surroundings? Was he wise in doing that? Why or why not?
- Do some students try to "paint themselves to blend in" here in our school? Why do you think they might do this? Do you think this is wise? What advice would you give them?
- Do you think twice-exceptional students are more likely to "paint themselves to blend in"? Why do you think they might do this?
- What enabled Eggbert to overcome the challenges he faced in his search for a place to live?
- How did the sun shining through a crack in the clouds change Eggbert's life? Have you ever had a special moment that inspired you to think differently about yourself? What happened?
- Why do you think Eggbert enjoyed traveling the world in search of famous cracked sights?

- Why do you think Eggbert sent the eggs back home in the refrigerator such beautiful postcards? What does that say about him? Would you have done that? Why or why not?
- How does Eggbert become proud of being slightly cracked?
- How are we "slightly cracked"? How do our cracks make us more interesting people? How do they help us?
- How can we celebrate our being "slightly cracked"?
- Eggbert travels to our school in search of interesting cracks. You have an opportunity to interview him. What questions would you ask? How might he respond?

Follow-Up Activities

- Write and illustrate a poem about Eggbert's journey to find a place to live.
- Create a classroom mobile that captures the lessons you learned through Eggbert.
- Create a photographic collage that celebrates Eggbert's special qualities.
- Write a rap about being slightly cracked.
- Design artistic postcards from new places that Eggbert might explore.
- Use your private journal to write a letter to Eggbert to let him know how you feel about what he did for himself and his friends back home in the refrigerator.
- Paint a picture of an egg that represents how you are slightly cracked. Highlight how your crack makes you unique.
- Write a text message to the eggs back home in the refrigerator. What would you want them to know about what you learned from Eggbert?

Thank You, Mr. Falker

Susan Grisanti and Jenna Wade were pleased with the lesson on *Eggbert*. They decided to extend their discussion with a second picture book, only this time they chose a childhood autobiographical account of Patricia Polacco, a beloved author of children's literature. Jenna and Susan believed that a carefully selected biography could strongly influence the life of a twice-exceptional child. They agreed that the person whose life story is being shared through biography could serve as a role model for intelligent children and assist them in thoughtful reflection on issues that challenged them. Jenna and Susan thought that Patricia Polacco's childhood account would speak directly to their students. Polacco's story is that of an artistic child who was challenged with dyslexia and dysnumeria and Mr. Falker, a young teacher who recognized her problem, designed an intervention to teach her how to read, and changed her life.

A Lesson Plan by Jenna and Susan

Overarching themes:

- Being twice-exceptional involves challenges
- Being twice-exceptional involves courage
- Overcoming a problem takes hard work
- Teachers can change lives

Discussion questions:

- What do we learn about young Trisha from her grandparents? How did they nurture her before she started school? How did they inspire her as a young girl?
- Do you think that Trisha was twice-exceptional? Explain your thinking.
- The author described Trisha's challenges with reading and explained, "when Trisha looked at a page, all she saw were wiggling shapes, and when she tried to sound out words, the other kids laughed at her" (p. 6). Do you think students in our school face this same challenge? Have you experienced this? If so, what was that like? What did you do?
- Trisha described reading as just plain torture. As a result, she turned to her love of art and spent much of her time drawing. Why do you think she did this? How do you think this may have helped her?
- Math was not much more fun as numbers were the hardest thing of all for Trisha to read. When the teacher said, "Line the numbers up before you add them," Trisha saw numbers that looked like a stack of blocks that were wobbly and ready to fall. Why do you think this was happening?
- Trisha's grandmother explains to her that "To be different is the miracle of life." What does she mean? What do you think of that message?

- Trisha was happy about her family's move to California because she thought maybe the kids in her new school wouldn't notice her struggles in learning. Do changes in schools help twice-exceptional students? Explain your thinking. Have you had experience with this? If so, what happened? How did that change affect you?
- Trisha had to deal with mean bullies. Why do you think bullies pick on kids like Trisha? What have you seen happening in your school? What advice do you have for students who get bullied?
- The author describes the new teacher, Mr. Falker. She says, "But right from the start, it didn't seem to matter to Mr. Falker which kids were the cutest. Or the smartest. Or best at anything." (p. 18). How would you feel about having Mr. Falker as your teacher? What can other adults learn from a young teacher like Mr. Falker?
- What were all of the ways that Mr. Falker encouraged and supported Trisha? How would Mr. Falker's style of teaching help you?
- When Trisha was mistreated by bullies, she retreated and hid under the inside stairwell where she felt safe. Do twice-exceptional students need safe havens in school? How might they discover them?
- Mr. Falker expressed some important thoughts to Trisha when he said:

> But, little one, don't you understand, you don't see letters or numbers the way other people do. And you've gotten through school all this time, and fooled many, many good teachers!... That took cunning, and smartness, and such, such bravery.
>
> (p. 30)

Why do you think he explained this to Trisha? How do you think she felt hearing those words from Mr. Falker? Can you remember a time when a teacher praised you for being smart and brave? How did you respond?

- What were the strategies that Mr. Falker used to teach Trisha how to read? Why do you think he was successful?
- When the story ended, Trisha was thinking of the important lesson that her grandfather had taught her, and she had tears of happiness roll down her cheeks. What was that lesson and what did it mean for Trisha? Have older family members passed on important lessons to you that have helped you in life? What were those lessons? How have they helped you? How might you share those lessons with other kids?

- In the introduction to her book, Patricia Polacco shared a letter written to teachers in which she described how Mr. Falker influenced her. She wrote:

> It was through his intervention and loving guidance that I was made aware that I was most certainly not dumb! His understanding changed my outlook and self-image. He showed me the joy of learning and helped me realize that anything is possible when there is no fear of failure.
>
> (p. 1)

- How will this message help teachers in their work with twice-exceptional students?

Follow-Up Activities

- Patricia Polacco, the author of this book, describes young Trisha as an artist who was able to make magic with her crayons. Using your crayons, draw two pictures. The first picture should represent Trisha's feelings at the beginning of the story when she has trouble with reading. The second picture should represent Trisha's feelings at the end of the story when she is successful at reading.
- When Mr. Falker arrives in school as the new teacher, the children notice that he wears "the neatest clothes." Design a new necktie for Mr. Falker to thank him for helping Trisha learn to read. Include a thank you note to attach to the gift box that holds his new tie.
- Design a safe place where twice-exceptional kids in your school can go when they are feeling overwhelmed. Where will this safe place be located? What will you include in that safe place that will help a student who is having a bad day?
- Design a television advertisement for celebrating great teachers like Mr. Falker.
- Design thank you posters for the teachers' lounge in your school.
- In your private journal, write about a time when you overcame a struggle with learning and describe how you felt about meeting that challenge.
- Write a letter to Trisha explaining how her story helped you to better understand yourself.

Jenna and Susan were pleased with the two lessons that they had created together and looked forward to co-facilitating the discussion with their students. With this planning completed, they realized they would continue to enjoy more collaboration. Combining their expertise and passion for teaching would enable them to continue addressing the affective needs of twice-exceptional learners.

Emily and Jalen Work Together to Nurture Resilience in Students

For multiple generations, Robert F. Kennedy Middle School had been a point of pride in the urban community. Parents consistently highlighted the hard work and success of dedicated teachers who worked relentlessly to address the complex needs of a diverse student body. Teachers at RFK understood that many of their students arrived at school every day from low-income households that faced difficult challenges. As a result, teachers and counselors knew that in order for RFK students to be successful, they needed to provide them with structured experiences and work in developing skills that would enable them to cope with the adversity in their lives.

Emily Walker taught seventh-grade language arts and social studies at RFK and was known for her dedication to students. Emily was the first in her family to earn a college degree and she had developed a real passion for teaching talented students from low-income backgrounds. In teaching honors classes, Emily worked with some of the brightest young people at RFK and often marveled at how many of them were able to look beyond their difficult circumstances and excel in school. Her personal background enabled her to develop a natural understanding of where they were coming from. Emily was fortunate to have a great working relationship with Jalen Thomas, an African American school counselor who also understood and appreciated the backgrounds of the students. Jalen had been working as both a counselor and coach at RFK for ten years and remained passionate about his work with young teens. Emily and Jalen worked well together, collaborating on facilitating social action projects in the community with their students and they were recognized by the school district for their efforts.

One morning before classes began, Emily stopped by Jalen's office. She wanted him to be aware of several of the challenges her students were

DOI: 10.4324/9781003235408-6

facing at home. She reported that Mateo, an eighth grader, had explained that he couldn't get his homework done the night before because of the "drama" that occurred at home over his older brother being arrested for driving under the influence. She also reported that Imani, Niesha, and Jackson were worried about their parents as they had lost their jobs due to the economic downturn. She expressed her concerns for Liam and Alejandra who were having difficulty remaining focused on their assignments as they worried about several undocumented family members being deported. Emily also let Jalen know that Kiara's mother had recently been diagnosed with breast cancer and although she had not observed a change in her academic performance, she was concerned about her overall emotional well-being.

Jalen listened closely as Emily described the issues her students were facing, and he assured her that he would check in on these students. Emily then asked if he would be willing to co-facilitate book discussions with her in her language arts classes. She had discovered several novels that featured teenagers overcoming serious adversity and she thought that Jalen would be ideal in helping her unpack important conversations that could be therapeutic for her students. Jalen was delighted that she had reached out to him and agreed to meet with her to discuss the young adult novels she had in mind. The following day after school, they met to begin preparing lessons. They had a great time exploring possible novels Emily had discovered and decided to focus on three: *Efrén Divided* by Ernesto Cisneros (2020), *The War That Saved My Life* by Kimberly Brubaker Bradley (2016), and *The Car* by Gary Paulsen (2006).

Efrén Divided

Emily and Jalen agreed that *Efrén Divided* by Ernesto Cisneros (2020) would be a great book to begin meaningful discussions with Emily's students. In this novel, 12-year-old Efrén Nava's world is overturned when he arrives home from school and he learns that his undocumented mother has been deported to Mexico. When his father takes on a second job to make ends meet, Efrén takes on the role of caregiver for his younger siblings. Though he feels unprepared to deal with the challenges he faces, his many talents enable him to make sure that Max and Mia feel safe and loved.

Emily's and Jalen's Lesson Plan

Overarching themes:

- Dedication to one's family
- Perseverance during times of adversity
- Cultural identity and pride
- The value of supportive friendships
- Having a belief in self

Discussion questions:

- What do you think of Efrén Nava as a big brother to Mia and Max? Would you enjoy having him as a brother?
- The Nava's family apartment was one large room. How might that have been difficult for a middle school student like Efrén?
- What was the relationship like between Max and Mia? Why do you think Efrén was very protective of the twins?
- How did the neighbors in Efrén's community support each other? How might this be important to Efrén and his family? Do you and your friends here at RFK Middle School experience this kind of support from your neighbors? If so, explain how.
- Jennifer Huerta shares a secret with Efrén about her parents being undocumented. How does that help Efrén?
- Jennifer shares an important Mexican saying: "They tried to bury us... but they didn't know we were seeds" (p. 21).
  How might that saying inspire the students in Efrén's school? How would it help?
- Efrén learns of his mother being deported back to Mexico. What do you think of his response? If you were Efrén's friend, what would you say to him during this difficult time?
- Efren explains how the presence of ICE in his community changed how people conducted their lives. What were some examples he shared? How do you think you would handle situations like these? What would you do?
- Efrén explained that Apá was his true hero. Why does he feel this way? Are there members of your family that you would consider your heroes? How do they inspire you?

- Efrén had to handle many responsibilities. What were they? How do you think he managed to juggle these responsibilities? Where do you think he got his strength to handle this? What kind of strength do you think that takes? Have you known of other teenagers handling the same kind of challenges that Efrén faced? What did they do?

- How does Efren convince his father to be part of the plan to get money to his mother across the border? What is his argument? Do you agree with him?

- The author of this novel Ernesto Cisneros wrote, "Going into Tijuana alone was something he had to do. For Amá. For the entire family…This was the only plan they had. He needed to be brave" (p. 96). What do you think of this statement?

- When Efrén shares the truth about his mother's deportation with Mr. Garrett, his teacher advises that he should only let his father handle the situation because this problem was too much to place on his shoulders. What do you think of Mr. Garrett's suggestion? How might you respond to Mr. Garrett?

- What does Efren learn about himself and his family's situation as a result of seeing the challenges and difficult conditions of the people in Tijuana?

- In observing life in Tijuana, Efrén reflected on the times that his parents had explained to him that they came to the United States "for a better life." What do you think Efrén is thinking about his parents' decision?

- Efrén observes families visiting with each other through the Muro – the iron barrier between Mexico and the United States. How does this influence his thinking? How do you think you would respond to such a situation?

- Efrén struggles with how much he can tell his friend David about his mother's deportation. Why is this so difficult?

- Efrén meets Lalo in Tijuana who helps him in many ways. What does he do for Efrén and his mother? How do friends help us during difficult times? How can we thank them?

- After his trip to Tijuana, Efrén felt connected to his Mexican side for the first time in his life. How is he feeling about his family's background and the way his parents raised him?

- The immigration officer at the border whispered to Efrén, "These forms represent a giant sacrifice from your parents. A true gift. Don't let it go to waste. Entiendes?" (p. 119). What does he mean? Do you agree? How do you think that statement might influence Efrén in the future?

- As Efrén's family prepares for Amá's homecoming, Apá expresses guilt about their living conditions and Efrén responds, "Apá – beds are over-rated. I don't need a bunch of fancy stuff to be happy. I've got my family...And that's more than a lot of people have. Trust me" (p. 127). What does that tell us about Efrén? How is this important?

- When the family learns that Amá is being held at a detention center, how does Efrén respond? How do you think he finds the strength to continue being so responsible?

- When the students discover the ugly words, "Deport Efrén Nava" are scribbled across his campaign poster, how does he respond? Why do you think he handles the situation this way? What do you think of his response to this event?

- What do you think of the way David describes the "favor" that Efrén paid him when he first arrived in the neighborhood? How does this cement their friendship?

- The author of this novel wrote, "And without saying another word, he leaned forward and gave his F-mon the longest bro hug the school had ever seen" (p. 141). Why was this significant to both David and Efrén?

- At the end of the novel, Efrén realizes that he and his siblings are now *Muro kids*, however, he decides that he will never give up on getting Amá home. He decides that "for all the semillitas like him, he couldn't stay buried any longer" (p. 143). What do you think of how he will approach the next chapter of his life? What can we learn from him?

Follow-Up Activities

- Efrén became responsible for preparing meals for his young siblings. Prepare a collection of easy-to-prepare Mexican recipes that teenagers can make when providing child care.

- Write a letter to the author Ernesto Cisneros to let him know what you learned about the challenges facing immigrant families from reading *Efrén Divided*.

- Design new campaign posters for Efrén's campaign at school. What are Efrén's personal qualities that you will highlight in the posters?

- Research Muro children online and write an editorial for your school newspaper about what you discover.

- Write a poem about Efrén's resilience.

- Using simple art materials, design an artistic sculpture to represent the lessons we learned from Efrén's family's experience.
- In your private journal, respond to the following prompt:
  How are you like Efrén Nava? How are your experiences similar to Efrén's? What have you learned from his story that will help you in the future?

The War That Saved My Life by Kimberly Bruker Bradley

Since Emily taught both language arts and social studies, she knew that infusing historical fiction into her curriculum was appropriate and Jalen Thomas agreed. They selected Kimberly Bruker Bradley's (2016) *The War That Saved My Life*. In this novel, Ada Smith, a ten-year-old, is experiencing her childhood in isolation. Born with a clubfoot and told by her mother that she is a worthless cripple, she is not allowed to leave the family's one-room apartment in London. As the horrors of the Nazi regime wreak havoc in Europe, an order from the government directs an evacuation of the children of London into the British countryside. Ada decides that she cannot allow her younger brother Jamie to go alone even though she has lived her entire life locked up in the family's apartment. In order to escape, Ada teaches herself to walk. Early one morning, the two children escape and soon are passed over by all of the residents who were supposed to take in evacuees. Lady Thorton, the head of the village's Women's Volunteer Service, takes the two children to Susan Smith. Miss Smith receives the children into her home where they remain for almost a year. Along with safety at home, Susan pursues the possibility of Ada undergoing surgery to correct her club-foot. Living in the country village of Kent is therapeutic for Ada as she heals from the years of abuse she suffered at her mother's hands. She learns to read, enjoys new friendships, and helps Susan overcome her own depression. She also cares for soldiers who are brought to the village and discovers a German spy in the village.

Her worst nightmare comes true when her mother is successful in taking the children away from Susan; however, the children are determined to return to Susan. During the German bombing of London, the children find Susan walking through the rubble in search of them. When they return to Kent, they discover that Susan's home has been destroyed by a bomb while she was searching for the children in London. All three realize that they have saved each other's lives.

Emily's and Jalen's Lesson Plan

Overarching themes:

- Emotional resilience
- Dedication to one's family
- Perseverance during times of adversity
- Finding emotional support from friends

Discussion questions:

- How can we understand the abusive treatment of Ada Smith's mother? What might influence a parent to behave this way? How do you think Ada was able to cope with her mother's treatment? How might children today respond to this kind of treatment by their parents?
- How did Ada teach herself to walk? How is this rather remarkable? What does this say about her personal strength?
- Ada explained that when things got really bad at home she would go away inside her head. What does she mean by that? Is this a good way to cope with adversity?
- In what ways does Ada use her intelligence to escape from the apartment with her younger brother Jamie?
- Ada escaped from her mother, Hitler's bombs, and her one-room prison. She felt free for the first time in her life. As she leaves London on the train, what advice would you want to give her?
- When Ada and Jamie arrive in the countryside, she discovers so much that she has never experienced before as a result of having been kept confined to the apartment so long. How do you think such isolation would affect a young girl like Ada? How does she overcome this?
- Ada has her first experience with a mirror. How does this affect her? What does she learn about herself?
- Ada is overwhelmed at times by her new life in the country with Susan. What are the many differences in her life that she must experience?

What does she learn? How do they help her to grow and become a stronger person?

- Susan advocated for Ada to be attending school because she believed that she was an intelligent girl. How did she discover that? Would you have joined Susan in her advocacy for Ada? Explain your thinking.
- When Jamie's teacher punished him for using his left hand, she pointed out that left-handedness was a mark of the devil. This led Ada to question whether her clubfoot was also a mark of the devil. How did the conversation with Susan help Ada?
- Ada showed her persistence by learning how to ride Butter the pony. In what other ways was Ada persistent? How does this quality help her in life? Can we develop persistence? How might it help us?
- How did Ada's relationship with Susan change over time? How do you think this helped Ada? How did it help Susan?
- When Butter's hoofs were trimmed by Fred Grimes, Ada's thinking about her clubfoot changed. How do you think this new knowledge helped her?
- Ada was overwhelmed by the movie theater's newsreel about the war. What does this tell us about her? Why do you think she had such a strong reaction?
- When Ada thought she had broken Susan's sewing machine she went into a serious panic. Why do you think she reacted that way? What does that tell us about her?
- After Jamie brought home a cat, his problem with wetting the bed ended. How do animals help us with stress in our lives? Have you known of people who own pets respond the same way? How were they helped?
- How does Ada's working in the stable eventually help her? Why do you think this is good for her?
- Ada thought of all the good things that had occurred since she and Jamie moved in with Susan. How did this help her?
- How did the first Christmas with Susan change Ada and her brother?
- In enjoying her new book, *Alice in Wonderland*, Ada reflected, "It was us. I thought. Jamie and me. We had fallen down a rabbit hole, fallen into Susan's house, and nothing made sense, not at all, not anymore" (p. 151).

  What does this passage mean to you? What do you think Ada is feeling? Why?

- How did Ada's friendship with Maggie influence her life? Have you experienced friendships during difficult times? What did they do for you?
- Why do you think Ada insisted on working with the Women's Volunteer Service in helping the wounded soldiers following the invasion of Dunkirk?
- Ada reflected, "There was a Before Dunkirk version of me and an After Dunkirk version. The After Dunkirk version was stronger, less afraid. It had been awful, but I hadn't quit. I had persisted. In battle I had won" (p. 175).
  What does this passage mean to you?
- How did Ada respond when she discovered the German spy? How does the police officer respond to her report? Why? What did she mean when she said, "my foot's a long way from my brain" (p. 190). How is that message meaningful in this story? How can we learn from this?
- When the spy was captured, Ada was celebrated as a hero in her village. How did this change her?
- How did Mam react to the changes in her children when she arrives to take them back to London? How did she treat Ada and Jamie? How did this treatment influence Ada's actions?
- Ada reflected, "At last I understood what I was fighting, and why. And Mam had no idea how strong a fighter I'd become" (p. 200).
  What do you think Ada meant by this?
- Before Ada and Jamie escape from Mam's apartment, Ada takes their birth certificates and other important papers she has discovered. Why was this important? What does this reveal about her?
- At the conclusion of the story, Susan says, "It's lucky I went after you. The two of you saved my life, you did" (p. 214). Do you agree with Susan? What do you think of Ada's reply, "So now we're even."

Follow-up Activities

- Using clippings from magazines, design a photographic collage that represents all of Ada's new learning experiences after being isolated for so many years.
- Ada, Jamie, and Susan came upon wartime posters that predicted victory in the war. Create an inspirational poster for your classroom that delivers an important message about overcoming difficult times.

- Research the experiences of children living in London during Hitler's Nazi regime. With the information you discover, write an entry in a London teenager's diary during those times.
- In your private journal, write a response to the following prompt: How did the war save Ada's life? How have difficult times in your life saved you?

The Car by Gary Paulsen

Following the historical fiction, Emily and Jalen decided to shift gears and offer the students a much different young adult novel that was both poignant and appealing to middle school students. Both Emily and Jalen thought that Gary Paulsen's (2006) *The Car* would really appeal to the boys in Emily's classes. In Paulsen's novel, the protagonist Terry Anders, a 14-year-old living in Cleveland, Ohio, is deserted when his two dysfunctional parents disappear. On his own, he occupies himself by assembling a car kit that has been collecting dust in the garage for years. When the car is completed, Terry is delighted when the car actually runs. Though he has no driver's license and does not know how to drive, he gets behind the wheel and begins to head west with plans to visit an uncle living in Oregon. His plans take a detour when Waylon Jackson joins him on the road. Waylon is an aging Vietnam veteran whose life experiences have been extraordinary. Eventually, Terry and his copilot meet up with Wayne Holz, a Harley Davidson biker and Waylon's friend from his time in Vietnam. Together the two men instill within Terry a new hunger to learn and experience different adventures in life. As a result, Terry ends up in locales as varied as a religious commune, a high-stakes poker game, and a visit to Custer's Last Stand. Through this exciting and sometimes dangerous journey, Terry learns a lot about people, overcoming tough circumstances, and ultimately, about himself.

Emily's and Jalen's Lesson Plan

Overarching themes:

- Developing internal strength
- Overcoming adversity

- Focused determination in pursuing a task
- Learning from new experiences
- Learning to trust individuals who are different
- Identity development in talented males

Discussion questions:

- What do you think of Terry's parents deserting him? What do you think of how Terry managed to survive on his own?
  Would students here at RFK be capable of handling this situation?
- What were the skills and talents that Terry had that enabled him to build The Blakely Bearcat? Where else do we see evidence of his giftedness? What are some of your favorite examples of Terry's intelligence in action?
- In what ways was Waylon Jackson talented? How did his talents help Terry along their journey?
- How did Terry learn to trust Waylon? How might you have responded to Waylon?
- Terry got lost in the driving and all he cared about was the highway ahead of him. How do you think that experience helped him? Have you ever had similar therapeutic experiences? Describe them.
- Waylon wanted to introduce Terry to his old friend Wayne for some automotive work. Do you think he wanted Wayne to help Terry in other ways?
- How do you think Waylon's and Wayne's experiences in Vietnam affected them, and how did it influence the way they chose to live their lives after the war?
- Waylon and Wayne discovered that Terry had much to learn. How did they convince him to develop more curiosity? How did Terry respond to their message? How did he change as a result of their teaching him to ask more questions?
- Waylon and Wayne led Terry to a series of new experiences: meeting Samuel, visiting a religious commune, a high-stakes poker game, and visiting Custer's Last Stand. How did the two men protect Terry during these adventures? What do you believe Terry learned from each of these experiences? How did they help him? Can you compare Terry's adventures to any learning experiences you have had that shaped you as a talented young person?

- At the beginning of his journey, Terry was rather cynical. But as time passed, he became more open to new people, new ideas, and new experiences. What do you think were the most important experiences he encountered that changed his perspective and why?
- How would you explain resilience? How were Waylon, Wayne, or Terry resilient?
- How do you think Terry Anders' journey traveling west in his new car helped him overcome the rejection by his parents?
- If you could travel anywhere, where would you go? What kind of transportation would you use to get there? What would you hope to see and do?

Follow-Up Activities

- When Terry was left on his own, he managed to feed himself from day to day. Prepare a collection of easy teen-friendly recipes for cooking meals for kids who may have to live alone for a while.
- Explore the internet in search of automobile car kits that may be available today. Research what would be involved in building a car from scratch.
- Sketch a picture of a car that you would enjoy building.
- Write the lyrics to a song describing Terry's adventure traveling west with Waylon and Wayne.
- Study an atlas of the United States and plan a car trip you would enjoy taking in the future. Write your detailed plan.
- In your private journal, write the letter that you would want Terry to send to his parents.
- Assume that Terry will one day connect with Waylon and Wayne again. How will he thank them for all they taught him? Design that thank you.

With the class having read and reflected on the three novels, Emily and Jalen planned to have the students analyze the responses of the three main characters in the novels and determine how Efrén, Ada, and Terry provided them with new ways of responding to challenges in their lives.

Jasmin Designs an Intervention for Gifted Black Males

Jasmin Young, a school counselor at Maple Grove Elementary School, sat at her desk nibbling on a sandwich she had packed for lunch. As she enjoyed the quiet time in her office, she gazed out her window looking out onto the school playground and watched the children enjoying their lunchtime recess. Her observations that day reminded her of a new project she wanted to take on. She noticed several Black boys on the playground teasing the younger children and she was reminded of recent conversations with teachers who had spoken to her about their concerns for some of the gifted Black boys in their classes. She reflected on those conversations about Tyrell Adams, Aiyden Moore, and Jalen Thomas. She was struck by how troubled the teachers were about these highly capable students who lately had not been taking school seriously. Comments such as, "Jalen hasn't turned in math homework for weeks, and I know he's the sharpest student in my class" and "Aiyden is all about becoming the class comedian lately." She thought back to the conversation about Tyrell, whose gifted education teacher expressed worry about his fluctuating motivation.

Ms. Young pondered the events of the day and reflected on how Black boys responded when they turned on the television and were exposed to some of the horrific experiences Black males were experiencing at the hands of police officers. She wondered about the conversations Black parents may have had concerning challenges their sons encountered outside of school. She was curious as to what the boys' thoughts were regarding the recent Black Lives Matter rally that had taken place downtown, whether or not they had attended, and how they might have felt about the event.

As she finished her lunch, she decided that she wanted to design an intervention for the gifted Black boys in school. She did not want to see highly capable boys like Tyrell, Aiyden, and Jalen lose their motivation and

DOI: 10.4324/9781003235408-7

not excel academically. Jasmin decided she would speak to third, fourth, and fifth-grade teachers after school and see if they wanted to recommend several Black young men from their classes to participate in a discussion group she would facilitate. As a school counselor, Jasmin had been trained in using high-quality literature to facilitate conversations with students about the challenges they encountered in their development. She decided a discussion group with gifted Black boys would be an experience she would enjoy and believed that exploring good books focused on issues that Black boys encounter would be one way to provide guidance to the most capable Black boys at Maple Grove. Jasmin had 30 minutes before her next meeting so she decided to browse through the media center in search of several books she knew she would want to explore with the students. She thought back to her recent counselor education conference where she had discovered some great new books that featured intelligent Black males and she hoped to locate those books in the school's collection.

In her conversations with teachers later that day, she had no difficulty obtaining a roster of names for the new group. Teachers at Maple Grove were definitely concerned about this special population of students and were pleased to learn of Jasmin's plan for an intervention. As she expected, Tyrell, Aiyden, and Jalen were all mentioned along with a substantial number of additional students. She knew that she needed to keep the group small, so she quickly realized that she might have to facilitate several groups. She would explain her plan to the principal and felt confident that Ms. Johnson would approve of her intervention. With the help of teachers, Jasmin would communicate with families before beginning the intervention and explain her objectives.

Jasmin decided she would begin the discussion group with an enjoyable warm-up activity to get acquainted with the boys. She would explain her plans for meeting regularly and would then read and discuss the book she had selected for the weekly session. She would then provide the boys time for follow-up activities. Her first selection was one of her favorite books by Derrick Barnes.

Crown: An Ode to the Fresh Cut by Derrick Barnes

In *Crown: An Ode to the Fresh Cut* by Derrick Barnes (2017), a Black teen describes his visit to the barbershop and explains how that experience influences how he feels about himself and how others view the fine young man he is. Watching the hardworking Black men in the barbershop, he is reminded about how he presents himself to the world. He tips the barber and leaves the shop with a fresh new cut and renewed self-confidence.

Jasmin read the book again and knew immediately that this selection was the perfect choice to introduce the discussion group. She was impressed with the poignant story the author shared and believed that the voice of Derrick Barnes would help her in conveying an inspirational message to the boys in her group. Jasmin became totally convinced of the significance of this book when she turned to the final page in the picture book and read "A Note from the Author" in which Barnes (2017) wrote:

> With this offering, I wanted to capture that moment when black and brown boys all over America visit "the shop" and hop out of the chair filled with a higher self-esteem, with self-pride, with confidence, and an overall elevated view of who they are. The fresh cuts. That's where it all begins. It's how we develop our swagger, and when we begin to care about how we present ourselves to the world. It's also the time when most of us become privy to the conversations and company of hardworking black men from all walks of life. We learn to mimic their tone, inflections, sense of humor, and verbal combative skills when discussing politics, women, sports, our community, and our future. And really, other than the church, the experience of getting a haircut is pretty much the only place in the black community where a black boy is "tended to" – treated like royalty.
>
> *Crown: An Ode to the Fresh Cut* focuses on the humanity, the beautiful, raw, smart, perceptive, assured humanity of black boys/sons/brothers/nephews/grandsons, and how they see themselves when they approve of their reflections in the mirror. Deep down inside, they wish that everyone could see what they see: a real life, breathing, compassionate, thoughtful, brilliant, limitless soul that matters – that desperately matters. We've always mattered. (p. 28)

Jasmin's Lesson

Overarching themes:

- The lives of Black young men matter
- Self-esteem, self-pride, and confidence in Black males
- How we present ourselves to the world
- Appreciating the many positive models of Black masculinity
- Celebrating the company of hardworking Black men from all walks of life

Discussion questions:

- Derrick Barnes, the author of this book introduces us to the story saying, "When it's your turn in the chair, you stand at attention and forget about who you were when you walked through that door." What does that mean to you? Are there other places other than the barbershop where you feel that way? What happens when you go there?
- Derrick Barnes says, "You come in a lump of clay, a black canvas, a slab of marble. But when my man is done with you, they'll want to post you up in a museum." What is he saying to Black young men? Do you agree? Have you ever had this experience? If so, how did you feel?
- Derrick Barnes writes, "It's amazing what a tight fade, high/low/bald does for your confidence: Dark Caesar." Have you ever transformed into a Dark Caesar in the barber's chair? What happened? What did you do?
- Mr. Barnes says that a fresh cut does something to your brain. He says, "It hooks up your intellectual." What do you think he means by that? Is this true?
- The author says that a fresh cut can make you feel like a brilliant, blazing star. Do you agree? Have you had that experience? If so, what was that like for you?
- Do girls in your school ever giggle and whisper sweet messages about you and your friends when they see your new hairstyle? If that has ever happened to you, tell us about how you responded. What did you do?
- The young teenager in the barbershop observes all of the older Black men who are also getting their haircuts. What does he notice about

them? Why is that important? What do you think he learns from watching the adult men in the shop? Have you watched older Black men in your community and learned from them? What did that do for you?

- Locs, cornrows, a faux-hawk, deep part, skin fade, "tapered sides," "a crisp but subtle line." What do those different styles do for boys like you? Which is your favorite? Why? What does that style do for you?

- How does the barber's witch hazel feel like "an electric stamp of approval"?

- Derrick Barnes says that the smile that appears on your face after a new haircut tells us that's "the gold medal you." What do you think the author means?

- The author points out that confidence from a new haircut may result in people responding to you in a positive way like your English teacher who hands you a paper with a "bright red 97 slapped on it" or your mother's look of love. Do people treat you differently when you present yourself with confidence? Describe that experience.

- Why does Derrick Barnes emphasize how important it is to tip the barber generously? What do you think he wants young men to understand? Why is this message important?

- When was the last time you felt "magnificent, flawless, like royalty"? Tell us about that moment.

- One person who wrote about this book described it by saying, "Oozes black cool." In your opinion, is that statement true? Share your thoughts.

- Another person said this book, "Allows young black men to feel like kings." How do you respond to this?

- Look up the word "ode" in the dictionary. What does it mean? Why do you think Derrick Barnes uses this word in the title of his book? What does it say to you about his message?

- If you could buy copies of this book to give to others, who would you share it with? Why? Why would it be important for them to read this book by Derrick Barnes?

Jasmin's Follow-up Activities

- Write a letter to Derrick Barnes. We will send it to his publisher to be sure he receives it. What would you say to him about the important lessons you learned from his book?

- Create a montage of photographs that represent what it means to be a gifted Black male.
- Design a poster for your school counselor's office that represents the important messages from *Crown: An Ode to the Fresh Cut*.
- Paint a picture that helps other kids in your school understand your talents.
- Create a photographic collection of all of the hairstyles that you have enjoyed. Be sure to include a caption for every picture.
- In your journal, write a letter to one important adult in your life who has helped you understand what it means to be a gifted Black male.
- Write a letter to the editor of our school newspaper about the lessons you learned from reading this book by Darrick Barnes.

After designing her first book discussion plan featuring the picture book by Derrick Barnes, Jasmin decided to incorporate literature written for students in upper elementary grades. She would reserve young adult literature for the sixth graders at Maple Grove. The second book she wanted to read with the group was *As Brave as You* by Jason Reynolds (2017).

As Brave as You by Jason Reynolds

Jasmin believed the group would enjoy *As Brave as You* in which Jason Reynolds describes the experiences of Genie and Ernie Harris, two brothers from Brooklyn who go to spend a month with their grandparents in rural Virginia where living is different. There is no cell phone reception! There are daily chores that have to get done. The brothers also have to spend time getting to know their grandparents much better. Ernie, the older brother is brave, confident, and cool while Genie is intellectual, often anxious, and afraid. Shortly after arriving, the brothers learn that their grandfather is blind. They are fascinated by how he matches his clothes, cooks with a gas stove, and even pours a glass of sweet tea without spilling it. Genie decides that his grandfather is the bravest man he has ever known. When Ernie turns 14, Grandfather Harris decides that in order to be a man, Ernie must learn to shoot a gun. Ernie has no interest in learning. Confused by his older brother's reluctance, Genie reflects on the meaning of being brave. He must answer the question: Is bravery becoming a man by proving something or is it more important to openly admit what you refuse to do?

Jasmin's Lesson

Overarching themes:

- Fear and bravery in adolescent boys
- Black masculinity across generations
- Guilt and forgiveness
- Admiration and respect for the elders in our families

Discussion questions:

- The author Jason Reynolds explained that Genie kept a small notebook and pen in his pocket so he could jot down interesting things that he wanted to Google, "because to Genie, the more questions you had, the more answers you could find. And the more answers you found, the more you knew." (p. 9). "Ernie, on the other hand, was the kind of kid who wore sunglasses 24/7 just to make sure everybody knew he was cool, and to him, the biggest mistake anyone could make was not to be" (p. 9). The author wants us to understand that the two brothers are very different from one another. How else were Genie and Ernie different? What do you think of these differences? Are you different from your siblings? If so, explain how.
- Which one of the two brothers would you want to have as a friend? Why?
- Before their trip, the Harris brothers thought that North Hill, Virginia, was going to be different from Brooklyn. What did they discover? How many ways was life in the country different from their life back home in the city? What did Genie and Ernie learn from these differences during their time with their grandparents? How do you think this helped them? Have you ever had similar experiences with your relatives? If so, what did you learn?
- Ernie and Genie ate grits for the first time while visiting their grandparents. What was their reaction? They also had sweet tea for the first time. How did they react to that? They also enjoyed soft shell crab sandwiches. What happens when we experience different foods and ways of living as we get older?
- Genie had an invitation from his grandfather to ask him all the questions he wanted to ask. His grandfather called their conversation an

"interview." What did Genie learn about his grandfather's life? What did he learn about his grandfather's blindness? Why was this important for Genie to learn? Have you ever had a chance to ask your older family members about their lives? If so, what did you learn? How did those conversations help you and your family?

- What are some of the important lessons that boys can learn from their grandfathers? Can you share an example from your experience with your grandfather or another older relative?

- When Genie learned that his grandfather's name was Brooke, how did he respond? Why was that discovery so important to him? How did this information help Genie think about himself? How might it change him?

- Genie writes many questions in his notebook every day. What are some of your favorite questions that he wanted to ask? What do these questions say about Genie?

- Genie discovers that his grandfather has many talents. What are the many ways Grandfather Harris shows us that he has special gifts and talents? Which of these impressed you the most? Why?

- Why do you think Grandfather Harris shares his secret *nunya bidness* room with Genie? When he says, "This room here...is my outside" (p. 74). What do you think he means? What does the secret room do for Grandfather Harris? How does it help him?

- Genie's grandmother says, "I see you boys are finally growin' your country legs. It don't take long to smarten up, does it?" (p. 118). What does she mean by that? Why is Genie confused by her comment?

- What do you think Genie thinks of his older brother's new friendship with Tess? Have you watched how your older brothers behave with their girlfriends? What have you learned from them?

- Genie observes conversations between his grandfather and his friend Crabtree. What do you think he learns from watching them? Have you ever studied how Black men interact with each other? If so, what have you learned from them?

- It's a tradition in North Hill, Virginia for a 14-year-old boy to learn how to shoot a rifle. On his 14th birthday, Ernie hesitates about his opportunity to learn this skill. Why do you think he struggles with this? What does it say about him? Have you ever been in a situation where other men were expecting you to do something you weren't comfortable with? What happened?

- Grandmother Harris pointed out to Ernie and Genie how their grandfather, their father, and their Uncle Wood were all brave in different ways. How do you think this influenced Genie's thinking about being scared?
- Grandmother Harris shared the letter that Uncle Wood wrote to her from Kuwait before he went into battle. Why do you think she wanted Genie to understand the men in his family? How would that help Genie?
- Grandfather Harris says to Ernie:

> I know you're scared...And here's what I want you to know. I'm scared sometimes too. It's funny...I've been livin' in the dark for a long time now, and sometimes it still scares me to death. But the times when I can't see old photos, or the letters from my oldest son, or I can't see that look of anger on your daddy's face, and now on yours, I think to myself that bein' blind ain't always so bad.
>
> (p. 196)

- What is the message that Grandfather Harris is trying to deliver to his grandsons? How will this message help them become better men?
- Grandmother Harris gave Uncle Wood's little red truck to Genie. Why do you think she did this? How do you think that made Genie feel? What do you think that special gift will do for Genie when he arrives back home in Brooklyn?
- Grandfather Harris gave Ernie his sunglasses. Why do you think he did this? How do you think that made Ernie feel? What do you think the sunglasses will do for Ernie when he returns home to Brooklyn?
- At the end of the story, Genie confesses to his grandfather. How do you think this confession made Genie feel? What did he learn about his grandfather's wisdom? How would this help him become a better young man?

Jasmin's Follow-Up Activities

- Write a letter to Jason Reynolds. We will send it to his publisher to be sure he receives it. What would you say to him about the important lessons you learned from his book?

- Grandfather Harris has designed his inside-outside room where he can spend quiet time in his private place. Design your personal inside-outside room where you can enjoy privacy and quiet time. What will you include in this safe space? Create an artistic sketch of your inside-outside room.

- Imagine that you are Ernie or Genie Harris, and you return to Brooklyn after having visited your grandparents. Write a letter to them to thank them for the time you enjoyed in North Hill, Virginia, and all the important lessons you learned from them.

- Write a poem that celebrates summer in the country.

- Write a rap about different kinds of bravery.

- Design a poster for your bedroom that captures all of the summer adventures that Ernie and Genie experienced in North Hill, Virginia.

- Create a word maze and incorporate all the words you can think of that highlight the important life lessons that Ernie and Genie learned in *As Brave as You*.

- Genie receives Uncle Wood's little red truck as a gift from Grandmother Harris. Using simple craft materials, create a memento that brings back important memories of time spent with your relatives and display it in your bedroom.

- Imagine you are Ernie or Genie returning to Brooklyn after your summer visit with your grandparents. You meet up with your best friends and share all the adventures that you enjoyed in Virginia. What will you tell them about life in the country, the interesting people you met, and the important lessons you learned. Role play that conversation with your friends.

- Follow Genie's example and begin collecting a notebook of important questions you want to explore.

Jasmin Young was excited about what she had planned. She knew there are many more books by Black authors she could share. She decided that the boys' responses to her first two selections would help her determine other books she would incorporate. As Jasmin looked forward to meeting with the boys, she began to think about other important books by Jacqueline Woodson, Walter Dean Myers, Nic Stone, Kwame Alexander, Christopher Paul Curtis, and Angie Thomas. The possibilities were endless!

Appendix
A Collection of Engaging Books

Picture Books

Penelope Perfect by Shannon Anderson (2015)
Key issues: Perfectionism; mistakes are part of life
Description: Penelope plans out every detail of every day because she likes things to be perfect. One morning her alarm clock doesn't go off and her world is turned upside down! How will she cope with a day of disaster where nothing goes according to plan?

Giraffes Can't Dance by Giles Andreae (2012)
Key issues: Building confidence; dance to the music you love
Description: Gerald the giraffe wants to learn how to dance. With his crooked knees and long thin legs, that's very difficult to do. When he attends the jungle dance, the other animals ridicule him. Feeling bad, he leaves the dance and receives some advice from an unlikely friend who explains that "Sometimes when you're different, you need a different song." With this understood, Gerald learns some great new dance moves!

Dancing in the Wings by Debbie Allen (2003)
Key issues: Determination in pursuing a dream; family pride and support
Description: Sassy is a very tall girl who always has something to say. She hopes to become a ballerina, but she worries that her long legs, large feet, and even her big mouth will keep her from her dream. When tiny girls in her ballet class mock her, she finds encouragement from her mother and Uncle Redd. A famous director visits

DOI: 10.4324/9781003235408-8

her school, sees her potential, and invites her to dance in a summer music festival.

Crown: An Ode to the Fresh Cut by Derrick Barnes (2017)

Key issues: Nurturing masculinity in young Black men; self-pride

Description: A young Black teen describes his visit to the barbershop and explains how that experience influences how he feels about himself and how others view the fine young man he is. Watching the hardworking Black men at the barbershop, he is reminded about how he presents himself to the world. He tips the barber and leaves the shop with a fresh new cut and renewed self-confidence.

I Am Every Good Thing by Derrick Barnes (2020)

Key issues: Having confidence and being proud of who you are; celebrating Black boyhood; building resilience

Description: A confident Black boy is proud of everything that makes him who he is. He has important plans and is determined to see them through. He's creative, adventurous, smart, polite, funny, and a trustworthy friend. Sometimes he falls and some days he's afraid, but he always gets right back up and conquers his fears.

Iggy Peck, Architect by Andrea Beaty (2007)

Key issues: Adult support of a child's passionate interest

Description: No one in second grade is better at building than Iggy Peck, who dreams of becoming a famous architect. Unfortunately, few people appreciate his talent, including his teacher. Iggy fears that he will have to trade his T-square for a box of crayons, but his situation changes after a significant class picnic that helps Iggy prove just how useful a talented builder can be.

Rosie Revere, Engineer by Andrea Beaty (2013)

Key issues: Pursuing a passion with persistence; overcoming failed attempts

Description: Alone in her room at night, Rosie builds great inventions made from odds and ends. Rosie's creations would amaze people if only she let anyone see them. Fearing failure and rejection, she hides them under her bed. When her Great Aunt Rose, a retired airplane designer visits, she teaches Rosie that a first "flop" isn't something to be embarrassed about – it's something to celebrate!

Ada Twist, Scientist by Andrea Beaty (2016)

Key issues: STEM girl power; the importance of perseverance and asking "why?"

Description: Ada Twist has always been very inquisitive, even when her fact-finding missions and sophisticated science experiments don't go as planned. She perseveres as she learns the importance of thinking her way through problems and continuing to remain curious.

Sofia Valdez, Future Prez by Andrea Beaty (2019)

Key issues: Children influencing change in their communities

Description: Every day, Abuelo walks Sofia to school until one morning he hurts his ankle at a local landfill. Sofia wonders what she can do about the dangerous Mount Trashmore. She is determined to convince her community to turn the mess into a family park. When she presents her plan to city officials, she's told that she can't build a park because she's just a kid. Can Sofia Valdez take on City Hall and win?

I Will Be Fierce! by Bea Birdsong (2019)

Key issues: Channeling the intelligence of young girls in positive ways

Description: A young girl decides to take on the challenges of her day like a brave explorer. She conquers the school library, forges new friendships, becomes a leader, and makes her voice heard. Her story is one of courage, confidence, kindness, and finding joy in everyday experiences.

Michael by Tony Bradman (2009)

Key issues: Behavior problems; precocity; underachievement; individuality

Description: Always late, always scruffy, and always misbehaving, Michael was the worst boy in school, but he surprises his teachers one day.

The Summer My Father Was Ten by Pat Brisson (1998)

Key issues: Relationships with others; coming of age; image management

Description: A girl's father recounts the tale of how his childish carelessness deeply bruised an elderly neighbor's well-being, and what he did to make things better.

Prince Cinders by Babette Cole (1997)

Key issues: Family relationships; creativity; image management; gender role expectations

Description: Prince Cinders is always forced to do the dirty work for his tough, strong, hairy older brothers until one day a well-intentioned fairy falls down his chimney and tries her best to grant his wishes.

Princess Smartypants by Babette Cole (2005)

Key issues: Gender role expectations; leadership

Description: Princess Smartypants outfoxes Prince Swashbuckle and convinces the people of the kingdom that she doesn't have to get married to live happily ever after.

Miss Rumphius by Barbara Cooney (1985)

Key issues: Individuality; gender role expectations; being alone; family relationships

Description: Alice Rumphius learns of faraway places from her grandfather at a very early age. As an older woman, she lives a complete life, traveling to many different parts of the world. She leaves the world a little more beautiful by leaving behind her garden of lupines.

Quiet by Tomie dePaola (2018)

Key issues: The benefit of mindfulness; enjoying the wonders of nature

Description: While enjoying a walk in the country, a loving grandfather imparts his gentle wisdom to his grandchildren. He reminds them that in a busy world, being quiet, still, and present with one another is a very special thing.

Agate by Joy Morgan Dey (2015)

Key issues: Celebrating individuality; self-acceptance and pride

Description: Agate is a moose who thinks of himself as a big brown mistake. He sees his friends as sparkling gems, beautiful, talented, and bright. When they see that he's feeling blue they remind him of a simple rule: be yourself and let others see the marvelous gem in you.

I Can Be Anything: Don't Tell Me I Can't by Diane Dillon (2018)

Key issues: The power of positive thinking; having high aspirations

Description: Zoe embraces the wonders of her world and its infinite possibilities. She declares, "I can be anything I want to be" and imagines herself becoming an archaeologist, a veterinarian, a musician, a famous chef, and more. But each time she dreams of a new possibility, she hears a little voice, presumably her own, who challenges her aspirations. Zoe's determination prevails until she finally decides that learning to read and reading a lot will help to pave her way to reaching her dreams.

Paul and Sebastian by Rene Escudie (1994)

Key issues: Being labeled "different"; relationships with others

Description: Paul's and Sebastian's mothers forbid them from playing together. Each parent insists that "they are not our kind of people." When the two boys become lost on a school field trip, they support each other until they are rescued. As a result, the boys' mothers realize the significance of their friendship and change their attitudes.

Weslandia by Paul Fleischman (2002)

Key issues: Being labeled "different"; creativity; image management; heightened sensitivity; individuality

Description: Entrepreneurial, creative Wesley stays true to himself when others want him to fit in. Eventually, his teasers and tormenters realize that conformity may not be the best way to go.

My Name is Not Isabella by Jennifer Fosberry (2010)

Key issues: Historical role models for gifted young girls

Description: Using her imagination, Isabella pursues an extraordinary adventure in which she travels with some of the inspirational women who changed history. She learns to appreciate strength, honor, determination, discovery, and unconditional love. Through this journey of discovery, Isabella also learns the importance of being her remarkable self.

My Name is Not Alexander by Jennifer Fosberry (2011)
Key issues: Historical role models for gifted young boys
Description: Using his imagination, Alexander pursues an extraordinary adventure in which he travels with some of the inspirational men who changed history. He discovers how great men become heroes and learns to see the importance of courage, creativity, pride, determination, and unconditional love. Through this journey of discovery, Alexander also learns the importance of being his remarkable self.

Wilfrid Gordon McDonald Partridge by Mem Fox (1995)
Key issues: Heightened sensitivity; relationships with others
Description: A young boy and an elderly woman share a warm relationship that allows them to appreciate the beauty of life together.

Elena's Serenade by Campbell Geeslin (2004)
Key issues: Creativity in young, gifted girls; gender role expectations; individuality
Description: Elena is a young girl in Mexico who learns to be a glass-blower and develops self-confidence.

Teammates by Peter Golenbock (1992)
Key issues: Coping skills; peer relationships; athletic giftedness
Description: The story of the friendship between Jackie Robinson and Pee Wee Reese of the 1947 Brooklyn Dodgers has several important messages for young men.

Woolbur by Leslie Helakoski (2008)
Key issues: Free-spirited children enjoying their unique approach to life
Description: Woolbur is not like other sheep. He hangs out with wild dogs, cards and spins his own wool, and even dyes it blue. When his parents try to get Woolbur to follow the flock, the other sheep decide to follow Woolbur!

Chrysanthemum by Kevin Henkes (1996)

Key issues: Image management; family relationships; peer relationships

Description: As she enters kindergarten, Chrysanthemum's once-perfect name seems to her less than ideal when her classmates begin to tease her relentlessly.

Eyes That Kiss in the Corner by Johanna Ho (2021)

Key issues: Cultural pride; self-acceptance; learning to love one's heritage

Description: A young Asian girl notices that her eyes look different from her friends'. They have big round eyes and long lashes. She recognizes that her eyes look like her mother's, her little sister's, and her grandmother's – eyes that kiss in the corners. Her family's eyes glow like warm tea and are filled with stories of the past and dreams of the future. As she draws from the strength of these important women in her life, she recognizes her own beauty and discovers a path to self-empowerment.

Amazing Grace by Mary Hoffman (1995)

Key issues: Individuality; theatrical giftedness; leadership

Description: Grace loves stories. She acts out the most exciting parts of all sorts of tales. So, when there is a chance to play a part in Peter Pan, Grace knows exactly what she must do. Grace's classmates are doubtful, but with the support of her wise grandmother who bolsters her independence, she gives an amazing performance.

Sweet Clara and the Freedom Quilt by Deborah Hopkinson (1995)

Key issues: Creativity; leadership; culturally diverse learners

Description: Clara, a young slave in the South, stitches a quilt with a map pattern that guides her to freedom in the North during the Civil War.

My Great-Aunt Arizona by Gloria Houston (1997)

Key issues: Gender role stereotypes; being alone; relationships with others; creativity

Description: Raised as an only child in Appalachia, Arizona spends her time outdoors, exploring and reading, and eventually becomes the most influential teacher the town has ever encountered.

Like Jake and Me by Mavis Jukes (2005)

Key issues: Heightened sensitivity; positive role models; family relationships

Description: A young boy comes to terms with a stepfather whose cowboy style is much different from his own.

The Invisible String by Patrice Karst (2018)

Key issues: Connection as a human need for all

Description: When a mother tells her two young children that they are all connected by an invisible string, the children probe further. Mom explains that an invisible string is made of love and even though you may not see it, you can feel it in your heart. Love is the unending connection that binds us all.

The Story of Ferdinand by Munro Leaf (2007)

Key issues: Heightened sensitivity; gender role expectations

Description: Ferdinand the bull does not butt heads with the other bulls in the pasture, yet he is chosen to appear in the bullring against the mighty matador. He decides he cannot be fierce and fight the matador. Instead, he would rather remain in the pasture smelling flowers.

Speak Up, Molly Lou Melon by Patti Lovell (2020)

Key issues: Using one's voice to protect others; bullying

Description: Molly Lou Melon's mother taught her that she can use her loud voice for good and to speak up for what's right. When school begins and a bully starts teasing everyone, including a new kid, Molly Lou knows just what to do. From standing up for a friend and admitting when she has had a mistake, Molly Lou shows everyone that speaking up is always the best choice.

Josefina Javelina: A Hairy Tale by Susan Lowell (2005)

Key issues: Pursuing your dreams; creativity and problem solving in gifted girls

Description: Josefina, a javelina with a dream of becoming a famous ballerina, journeys to California in the hope of being discovered. Eventually, she finds a special place where her talent is appreciated.

Harrison-Dwight: Ballerina and Knight by Rachael MacFarlane (2018)

Key issues: Challenging gender expectations; encouraging individuality; expressing one's feelings

Description: As Harrison-Dwight enjoys each and every day filled with adventures and fun, he experiences a variety of emotions. He feels sadness, joy, pride, fear, anger, and courage. He sends empowering messages that encourage creativity, individuality, and freewheeling fun and teaches us that it's okay to express what we're feeling inside.

Tomas and the Library Lady by Pat Mora (2000)

Key issues: Culturally diverse learners; positive role models; creativity

Description: Tomas, the young child in a family of migrant workers, develops a meaningful relationship with the librarian as he falls in love with books.

The Boy Who Was Raised by Librarians by Carla Morris (2007)

Key issues: Having a passion for learning; finding supportive mentors

Description: Melvin discovers that the public library is the place where he can discover the answers to so many of the questions he asks. In doing so, he becomes friends with three dedicated librarians who support him in his quest for knowledge.

The Proudest Blue: A Story of Hijab and Family by Ibtihaj Muhammad & S. K. Ali (2019)

Key issues: Being proud of one's cultural heritage; unbreakable bonds between siblings

Description: Faizah knows that the first day of school will be special because it's her older sister Asiya's time to celebrate wearing her first-day hijab made of beautiful blue fabric. She understands how this first day of wearing a hijab is important as her mother explained that it means being strong. When students ridicule her sister, Faizah is reminded of her mother's message, "If you understand who you are, one day they will too" and she remains strong in supporting her sister, a princess in a hijab.

Stephanie's Ponytail by Robert Munsch (1996)

Key issues: Image management; peer relationships; leadership

Description: Stephanie shows up to school each day with a different hairdo, and every subsequent day the whole class has copied her look. She finds a way to maintain her uniqueness while teaching her classmates a lesson on conformity.

The Paper Bag Princess by Robert Munsch (2005)
Key issues: Image management; gender role expectations; individuality
Description: Elizabeth, a strong-willed young princess, fights off a dragon and decides not to marry the arrogant, shallow-minded Prince Ronald.

The Recess Queen by Alexis O'Neill (2002)
Key issues: Schoolyard bullies
Description: Mean Jean is a bully on the school playground. A new girl named Katie Sue arrives and becomes the new recess queen by being nice to everyone including Jean.

Coat of Many Colors by Dolly Parton (1996)
Key issues: Creativity; family relationships; individuality
Description: A poor girl celebrates her coat of many colors, made by her mother from rags. Despite the ridicule of other children, she cherishes the coat that was made with love.

The Big Orange Splot by Daniel Pinkwater (1999)
Key issues: Creativity; identity development
Description: Mr. Plumbean lived on a street where all the houses were identical. When a seagull drops a big splot of orange paint on the top of Mr. Plumbean's home, he decides to paint his house to represent his life dreams. When his neighbors resist his ideas, he succeeds in slowly convincing them to do the same and the neighborhood becomes a far more interesting place where people are comfortable expressing their individuality.

Pink and Say by Patricia Polacco (1994)
Key issues: Culturally diverse learners; peer relationships; individuality; leadership; developing a value system
Description: Pink, an African American Union soldier in the Civil War, discovers a seriously injured Say, a White teenage soldier, and takes him home to make him well.

Appelemando's Dreams by Patricia Polacco (1997)

Key issues: Creativity; leadership; being labeled "different"; perseverance

Description: Appelemando spends his time enjoying vivid daydreams, and the villagers are convinced that he will never amount to much. Eventually, his colorful dreams change the village and all the people living in it.

Thank You, Mr. Falker by Patricia Polacco (2012)

Key issues: Gifted/learning disabled; relationships with others; perseverance; artistic giftedness

Description: An autobiographical account of an artistic fifth grader's struggle to learn to read.

Mrs. Katz and Tush by Patricia Polacco (2009)

Key issues: Positive role models; culturally diverse learners; perseverance

Description: A young African American child and his older Jewish neighbor establish a lifelong friendship.

My Papi Has a Motorcycle by Isabel Quintero (2019)

Key issues: Cultural pride; father-daughter relationships

Description: Every day when Daisy Ramona's father comes home from his construction job, she grabs her helmet, and he takes her for a ride on his motorcycle. As they zoom around their neighborhood on his bike, she sees the people and places she loves. She observes a vibrant community that is rapidly changing. As she enjoys the evening sunsets, she celebrates her home and her father's love.

The Dot by Peter Reynolds (2003)

Key issues: Individuality; creativity; self-expression through art

Description: When Vashti becomes frustrated in her elementary art class and announces that she simply cannot draw, her clever teacher succeeds in convincing her to experiment and enjoy self-expression.

Ish by Peter Reynolds (2004)

Key issues: Individuality; creativity

Description: A single reckless comment from an older brother turns a young boy's artistic expressions into painful struggles. A younger sister helps him to recognize and appreciate the unique quality in his creativity.

Tar Beach by Faith Ringgold (1996)

Key issues: Individuality; culturally diverse learners; perseverance

Description: Cassie Louise Lightfoot, eight years old in 1939, has a dream to be free to go wherever she wants to for the rest of her life. One night, on the "tar beach," the rooftop of her family's Harlem apartment, her dream comes true. She learns anyone can fly – "All you need is somewhere to go you can't get to any other way."

An Angel for Solomon Singer by Cynthia Rylant (1996)

Key issues: Being alone; image management; relationships with others

Description: Homesick for the Midwest, Solomon Singer spends his days in New York City unhappy and dreaming of a better life. One night, he strolls into a special diner and eventually realizes that, once you find a friend, everything else tends to fall into place.

After the Fall: How Humpty Dumpty Got Back Up Again by Dan Santat (2017)

Key issues: Resilience; confronting your fears

Description: Humpty Dumpty shares an inspiring epilogue to his classic story. Humpty lost his courage and his spirit of adventure after he fell off the wall and cracked up. He surprises everyone when he learns an amazing new talent. He now encourages all of us to overcome fears, learn to get back up, and reach new heights.

Katie's Cabbage by Katie Stagliano (2015)

Key issues: Sensitivity and empathy; leadership talent; the benefits of service to others

Description: Katie's third-grade teacher provides her classmates with cabbage seedlings. Katie devotes much tender loving care and harvests a 40-pound cabbage that she takes to a soup kitchen to feed families in need. Her experience volunteering in the kitchen inspires her to organize her friends to maintain vegetable gardens and donate the harvests to feed the hungry.

Dear Mrs. LaRue: Letters from Obedience School by Mark Teague (2002)

Key issues: Underachievement, individuality; creativity

Description: Doggy Ike's owner sends him to obedience school to change his behavior. Ike attempts to get his way out of the stifling environment and tries to have Mrs. LaRue see that he's OK the way he is.

Alexander and the Terrible, Horrible, No Good, Very Bad Day by Judith Viorst (2009)

Key issues: Dealing with stress; coping skills

Description: The trials and tribulations in a young boy's daily life can sometimes be stressful.

Rosie and Michael by Judith Viorst (1988)

Key issues: Peer relationships; gender role expectations

Description: Rosie and Michael are the best of friends. They know they can depend on each other. They can even tell what they like about each other – even the bad things!

Nana Akua Goes to School by Tricia Elam Walker (2020)

Key issues: Celebrating cultural differences; children with immigrant family members

Description: It is a special day at Zura's elementary school – a day to introduce grandparents and celebrate what makes them special. Aleja's grandfather is a fisherman and Bisou's grandmother is a dentist. Zura's Nana, who is her favorite person in the world, looks a bit different from other grandmothers. Nana Akura is from Ghana and was raised in the old West African tradition of wearing tribal markings on her face. Zura is hesitant to bring Nana to school because she is worried that her classmates will make fun of her. Nana knows what to do. With a quilt of traditional African symbols and a bit of face paint, Nana Akua describes what makes her special and is able to make all of Zura's classmates feel special too.

Odd Velvet by Mary E. Whitcomb (1998)

Key issues: Image management; creativity; being alone; peer relationships

Description: Velvet doesn't exactly fit in, but soon she is able to show her classmates just how empowering it can be to simply be yourself.

Galimoto by Karen Lynn Williams (1995)
Key issues: Perseverance; creativity; culturally diverse learners; family relationships
Description: Kondi, a young African boy, is determined to make a galimoto – a toy vehicle made of wires. His brother laughs at his idea, but all day long Kondi gathers the wire he needs. By nightfall, his wonderful galimoto is ready for the village children.

The Boy Who Grew Flowers by Jen Wojtowicz (2005)
Key issues: Being labeled "different"; empathy in gifted children
Description: A young boy is shunned at school because he sprouts flowers every full moon. He makes a distinctive pair of shoes for a classmate who appreciates his special abilities.

A Quiet Place by Douglas Wood (2005)
Key issues: Being alone; identity development; creativity
Description: A vivid description of the special places that a child can go to be quiet, to be alone, and to imagine.

The Day You Begin by Jacqueline Woodson (2018)
Key issues: Finding a place where you belong; the courage it takes to be oneself
Description: There are many reasons that young children may feel different when they arrive in a new school. It may be how they look or talk, where they are from, or what they eat. What does it take for children who feel different to share their stories? This inclusive story encourages children to discover the beauty in their own lives and share it with others. By doing so, they will be able to find someone a little bit like them.

Literature for Elementary Grades 3–5

Crenshaw by Katherine Applegate (2015)
Key issues: Creative resilience of a child's mind can soften difficult times

Description: Jackson's family has fallen on tough times. There's no money for rent and little food. His parents, sister, and dog have to live in their minivan again. Jackson is frustrated with his parents who gloss over their problems with humor and don't deal with the reality of their situation. Crenshaw is a large imaginary cat that returns to Jackson's life to help him cope with his family. Can an imaginary friend really help? Skeptical Jackson tries to dismiss Crenshaw as a figment of his imagination, but the cat's words of wisdom start to make sense to him.

Ruby on the Outside by Nora Raleigh Baskin (2016)

Key issues: Children living with the incarceration of a parent; creativity and healing; embracing the goodness that surrounds us

Description: Ruby Danes is ready to begin middle school, and only her aunt knows her darkest secret: her mother is in prison. When Margalit Tipps moves into Ruby's neighborhood and the two girls get to know each other, Ruby believes she has found her first real friend. But can she tell Margalit the truth about her mother? A tragedy from Margalit's past surfaces with a worrisome connection to the event that put her mom in prison and she faces a real dilemma. Ruby understands that if she divulges her secret, she could lose what she cares about most.

The War That Saved My Life by Kimberly Brubaker Bradley (2015)

Key issues: Personal struggle for freedom; resilience

Description: Ten-year-old Ada has never been allowed to leave her one-room apartment in London because her abusive mother is too humiliated by her daughter's clubfoot. Her younger brother Jamie is sent to the British countryside to flee from the war and Ada manages to escape with him. When the children are taken into a home with Susan, Ada's life changes as she teaches herself to read and write, ride a pony, and look out for German spies. The children's bond with Susan grows but will it sustain them through wartime?

The War I Finally Won by Kimberly Brubaker Bradley (2017)

Key issues: Resilience; overcoming adversity

Description: In the sequel to *The War that Saved My Life*, Ada's clubfoot has been surgically fixed. She is no longer the damaged young girl her mother described. As World War II rages on, Ada, her brother, and their guardian Susan move into a home with another family. Life in the crowded cottage is tense and then Ruth, a Jewish girl from Germany, moves in. Could Ruth be a spy? Life during wartime grows more complicated and the family faces serious challenges. How will Ada keep fighting? How will she survive?

Because of Mr. Terupt by Rob Buyea (2010)

Key issues: Compassion for others who may be different; teachers who provide important life lessons

Description: School begins at Snow Hill School and seven very different students find themselves in Mr. Terupt's fifth-grade class. They don't have much in common and they've never gotten along but their new teacher helps them to find strength within themselves and in each other. When Mr. Terupt suffers a serious accident, his students must complete their fifth-grade experience without him. Will they be able to remember their strengths and the important lessons he taught them?

A Drop of Hope by Keith Calabrese (2019)

Key issues: Maintaining a positive view of life; the power of hope; significance of friendships

Description: Times are difficult and jobs are scarce in Cliffs Donnelly, Ohio. An old well has suddenly begun to grant wishes and three sixth graders are the only people in town who know why. Ernest believes that good deeds make magic happen. Ryan thinks they should mind their own business and Lizzy believes in facts, not fairy tales. When more wishes are made, the well's true secret becomes a challenge to keep, and Ernest, Ryan, and Lizzy discover they can give everyone a little hope, one wish at a time.

Efrén Divided by Ernesto Cisneros (2020)

Key issues: Challenges facing immigrant families; talented children as caregivers; love of family

Description: Twelve-year-old Efrén Nava's world is overturned when he arrives home from school and he learns that his undocumented mother has been deported to Mexico. When his father takes on a second job to make ends meet, Efrén takes on the role of caregiver for his younger siblings. Though he feels unprepared to deal with the challenges he faces, his many talents enable him to make sure that Max and Mia feel safe and loved.

The Landry News by Andrew Clements (2007)
Key issues: Creativity; perseverance; using one's talents for positive results; positive role models
Description: A fifth grader writes an editorial about her teacher that inspires many important changes at her school.

Waiting for Normal by Leslie Connor (2008)
Key issues: Coping with family challenges; searching for friendship; finding emotional support beyond one's family
Description: Addie must learn to understand her mother's erratic behavior and being separated by her loving stepfather and half-sisters when she and her mother move out to live on their own.

New Kid by Jerry Craft (2019)
Key issues: Identity development; racial pride; peer relationships
Description: In this timely graphic novel, Jordan Banks, a talented cartoonist, dreams of attending an art school. Instead, his parents enroll him in a prestigious private school known for strong academics. Not only is he far removed from his urban neighborhood, but he is also one of few kids of color in seventh grade. Torn between two worlds and struggling to fit in either one, can Jordan learn to negotiate his new school culture and remain true to himself?

Because of Winn-Dixie by Kate DiCamillo (2009)
Key issues: Image management; family relationships; coping skills
Description: Because of an ugly, cheerful dog named Winn-Dixie, ten-year-old Opal learns to connect with those around her as she finally begins to cope with the fact that her mother abandoned her several years ago.

Beverly, Right Here by Kate DiCamillo (2019)
Key issues: Unexpected friendships; identity development; independence in gifted young women

Description: Beverly Tapinski has run away from home many times, but this time she is simply leaving her dysfunctional mother and painful memories. She is determined to survive on her own and succeeds in finding a job and a place to live. Beverly does not want to depend on others and have others depend on her. Despite her efforts, she ends up making important connections with people around her and learns to appreciate a new view of herself through their eyes.

Blended by Sharon M. Draper (2019)
Key issues: Blended families; biracial identity development; microaggressions; racial profiling
Description: Eleven-year-old Isabella's parents are divorced so she lives in two worlds. One week she's Isabella living in an affluent neighborhood with her Black father, his girlfriend Anastasia, and her son Darren. The next week she's Izzy with her White mother and her boyfriend John Mark, in a modest home that she loves. Torn between the two homes and attempting to understand her identity as a biracial child, her parents both become engaged at the same time. Isabella deals with more family conflict. She wonders if she will ever be able to bring her two worlds together, until the worst happens.

Nobody's Family Is Going to Change by Louise Fitzhugh (2016)
Key issues: Gender role expectations; family relationships
Description: Emma, who is very intelligent, wants to become a lawyer. Her seven-year-old brother, Willie, wants to become a dancer. Their father is opposed to both of these career choices.

Joey Pigza Loses Control by Jack Gantos (2002)
Key issues: Living with attention deficits; father-son relationships
Description: With new medications, Joey believes his attention deficit disorder is under control and he can begin to live like a normal kid. He convinces his skeptical mom to let him spend part of his summer visiting his estranged father. The problem Joey faces is that his dad is just as wired as Joey used to be and believes Joey can deal with his ADD without the help of drugs. Is being friends with his father worth losing his self-control?

My Side of the Mountain by Jean Craighead George (2004)
Key issues: Coming of age; individuality; being alone
Description: A young man's experiences of life in the wild provide him
with an opportunity to learn about the wilderness, and himself, in
the process.

Julie of the Wolves by Jean Craighead George (2004)
Key issues: Image management; family relationships; being alone;
perseverance
Description: Miyax rebels against a home situation that she finds intol-
erable. She becomes lost in the Alaskan wilderness, without food
or a compass. She survives day to day and is forced to redefine the
traditional richness of Eskimo life.

When Life Gives You Mangos by Kereen Getten (2020)
Key issues: Finding courage to face the truth; honest, spirited, and
authentic girls
Description: Clara, a 12-year-old island girl lost her memory of a storm
that occurred the summer before. Because of this, she is teased by
her friends and the whole village constantly argues about her. She
learns the truth about what transpired during the hurricane and
moves forward with her childhood.

Pictures of Hollis Woods by Patricia Reilly Giff (2004)
Key issues: Identity development; positive role models; creativity; artistic giftedness
Description: Artistically talented Hollis Woods has a history of running
away from foster homes. She discovers a place where she wants
to remain. There she bonds with Josie, her new guardian, who is a
slightly eccentric, retired art teacher. Through her sketchbook, she
preserves her memories, develops an understanding of her fears,
and experiences catharsis as she searches for a place where she
belongs.

The Liberation of Gabriel King by K. L. Going (2007)
Key issues: Cross-cultural friendships; overcoming fear
Description: Gabriel King is afraid of just about everything, includ-
ing spiders, loose cows, and moving on to fifth grade. Gabe's best

friend, Frita Wilson, thinks Gabe needs some liberating from his fears. Frita knows something about being brave – she's the only Black kid in school in a town with an active KKK. Together, Gabe and Frita spend the summer confronting what scares them most.

Philip Hall Likes Me. I Reckon Maybe by Bette Greene (1999)
Key issues: Gender role expectations; peer relationships
Description: Beth Lambert could easily be the best student in her class if she did not let Philip Hall, her first love, have this distinction.

The Gift-Giver by Joyce Hansen (2005)
Key issues: Gender role expectations; multicultural learners; image management; perseverance; peer relationships
Description: Gifted loner Amir moves to an inner-city neighborhood and teaches Doris, another gifted Black student, and other peers how to feel better about themselves and how to appreciate everyone's talents.

Ida B by Katherine Hannigan (2004)
Key issues: Giftedness and creativity in young girls; coping with family challenges; emotional support from teachers
Description: Fourth-grader Ida B enjoys being homeschooled and playing in her family's apple orchard until her mother begins treatment for breast cancer and her parents must sell part of their Wisconsin farm and send her to public school.

Crossing the Wire by Will Hobbs (2007)
Key issues: Overcoming adversity and developing resilience; belief in self
Description: When falling corn prices in Mexico threaten his family with starvation, 15-year-old Victor Flores heads north to cross the wire into the United States so he can find employment and send money home. Victor's journey is filled with near-death situations as he must decide whom to trust. Through his desperate struggle, Victor learns much about courage and the love of family.

Fish in a Tree by Lynda Mullaly Hunt (2017)
Key issues: Challenges of dyslexia; overcoming bullies

Description: Ally is smart in finding ways to hide her inability to read. She creates clever and disruptive distractions; however, she does not fool Mr. Daniels who sees the creative kid underneath her troublemaker façade. With his help, she learns not to be so tough on herself and comes to understand that dyslexia is nothing to be ashamed of. She discovers that great minds don't necessarily think alike and there is more to her than a label.

Baseball Fever by Johanna Hurwitz (2000)
Key issues: Parental expectations; family relationships; coping skills
Description: The only game Ezra's father has any respect for is chess; he cannot understand why his son would rather rot his brain watching baseball than reading a book. How can Ezra ever convince him that cheering for a national pastime isn't completely off base?

Mango Delight by Fracaswell Hyman (2017)
Key issues: Maintaining authentic friendships; coping with instant adulation; parental expectations for gifted girls; discovering outlets for one's talents
Description: When seventh-grader Mango Delight Fuller accidentally breaks her best friend's new cell phone, her middle school life becomes high drama. She loses her friends and her spot on the track team and even costs her father his job as a chef. When her ex-friend sneakily signs up Mango to audition for the school musical, her plan backfires as Mango wins the lead role and soon becomes a YouTube sensation. This attracts the attention of the school's queen bee. Mango finds herself forced to make choices about the kind of friend she wants to have, and more importantly, the kind of friend she wants to become.

The Phantom Tollbooth by Norton Juster (2007)
Key issues: Creativity; image management
Description: In this delightful classic, Milo learns that, as long as you have an active imagination, life will never be boring.

Hello, Universe by Erin Entrada Kelly (2020)
Key issues: Being different; finding your inner strength; unexpected friendships

Description: Virgil Salinas is shy and kindhearted and feels out of place in his loud family. Valencia Somerset is deaf, smart, brave, secretly lonely, and loves nature. Kaori Tanaka is a self-proclaimed psychic with a little sister Gen who follows her around. Chet Bullens wishes all these weird kids would just quit being so different so he could concentrate on basketball. When hateful Bullens pulls a prank that traps Virgil and his pet guinea pig at the bottom of a well, this crisis leads Kaori, Valencia, and Gen on an epic quest to find missing Virgil. With bravery, quick thinking, and a little bit of help from the universe, their rescue happens, friendship blooms, and a bully learns an important lesson.

From the Mixed-Up Files of Mrs. Basil E. Frankweiler by E. L. Konigsburg (2007)

Key issues: Parental expectations; family relationships; image management

Description: Tired of being "Straight A's Claudia Kincaid," Claudia persuades her brother to run away with her. They run away to the Metropolitan Museum of Art for a week where they solve a number of mysteries and learn about themselves in the process.

The View from Saturday by E. L. Konigsburg (2007)

Key issues: Positive role models; peer relationships; creativity; individuality

Description: Four sixth graders, with their own individual gifts and talents, develop a special bond when they are recruited by their teacher to represent their class in an Academic Bowl competition.

Ungifted by Gordon Korman (2014)

Key issues: Channeling one's talents in positive directions

Description: After Donovan Curtis pulls off a major prank in his middle school, he isn't disciplined. Instead, he's sent to the Academy of Scholastic Distinction, a special program for gifted and talented students! ASD is the perfect hideout for a prankster like him. When students and teachers there realize that Donovan may not be great at science or math, he proves that his gifts and talents may be exactly what ASD kids never realized they needed.

Restart by Gordon Korman (2017)

Key issues: Bullying; moral development

Description: Chase Ambrose does not remember falling off the roof or hitting his head. His memory is gone! He wakes up in a hospital room and suddenly has to learn his entire 13-year life over again. He's Chase, the guy with amnesia, but who is he? He's learning stories of the super jock and bully who maintained a reign of terror over his entire middle school. Is that the person he is or is it possible to get a clean start?

A Wrinkle in Time by Madeleine L'Engle (2007)

Key issues: Creativity; image management; family relationships

Description: A search for a missing parent, involving a fantasy, becomes a search for identity for both a young boy and his sister.

Anastasia Krupnik by Lois Lowry (2009)

Key issues: Leadership; creativity

Description: Anastasia Krupnik is left in charge of her very disorganized family. She invents the Krupnik Family Nonsexist Housekeeping Schedule and saves the day.

Athlete vs. Mathlete by W. C. Mack (2013)

Key issues: Sibling rivalry; identity development; changes in family dynamics

Description: Owen Evans and his twin brother Russell couldn't be more different. Owen lights up the scoreboards while Russell lights up math class. They have gotten along well by going their separate ways, but will that change? The new basketball coach recruits Russell to the seventh-grade team and Owen has to compete to stay in the game. When another student tries to take Russell's position of captain of the mathlete team, will the two brothers support each other or will they be sidelined?

Be a Perfect Person in Just Three Days! by Stephen Manes (2018)

Key issues: Perfectionism; peer relationships; coping skills

Description: Milo Crinkley learns that it's OK to be less than perfect.

Merci Suárez Changes Gears by Meg Medina (2018)

Key issues: Transitions to middle school; bullying, love, and pride of intergenerational families

Description: Merci Suarez expected that middle school would be different, but she never imagined how being a scholarship student in a private school would change her life. She is assigned the responsibility of being a Sunshine Buddy to another new kid in school, the new handsome hunk of sixth grade. As a result, Merci becomes the target of other jealous sixth-grade girls. While negotiating her new school's culture and challenges from her peers, she must also manage the changes at home as her extended family must face the declining health of Merci's beloved grandfather.

The Stars Beneath Our Feet by David Barclay Moore (2017)

Key issues: Overcoming the loss of a loved one; using one's creativity to heal; pursuing a passion; appreciating autistic classmates

Description: Twelve-year-old Lolly Rachpaul is trying to steer a safe path through the projects in Harlem in the wake of his older brother's gang-related death. A family friend brings him a gift of two enormous bags filled with Lego bricks and his situation begins to change as Lolly builds a fantasy-like Lego city at the after-school community center. His creativity and perseverance enable him to overcome the loss of his brother, build a bridge to an autistic new friend, and find a supportive community that celebrates his talents.

Darnell Rock Reporting by Walter Dean Myers (2008)

Key issues: Building self-confidence; being proud of one's talents

Description: Darnell Rock isn't the kind of kid who volunteers to be a school newspaper reporter. It sounds like homework! But this may be his last chance to make a positive contribution to his school. Although he'd much rather be hanging out with his friends, he gets interested in the *Oakdale Gazette*. He discovers that people actually pay attention to the words he writes and begins to believe in his abilities.

It Ain't All for Nothin' by Walter Dean Myers (2009)

Key issues: Moral development

Description: Life in Harlem isn't easy for Tippy, but he and his Grandmother Carrie are doing okay. When his grandmother gets sick, Tippy has to move in with his father Lonnie, who doesn't have much time in his life for a son he barely knows. Tippy has to decide whether he is willing to negotiate the fine line between right and wrong. Grandma Carrie said if he had Jesus in his heart, there wasn't anything to worry about, but for Tippy, it's not that simple.

Me, Mop, and the Moondance Kid by Walter Dean Myers (2009)

Key issues: Powerful friendships; emotional sensitivity and empathy; resilience

Description: T. J., his younger brother, Moondance, and Mop – Miss Olivia Parrish – grew up together in an orphanage. They are family. Now that T. J. and Moondance have been adopted, and Mop has to find a new family before the orphanage closes, Mop hopes that if she can play catcher for the Little League baseball team that they all belong to, the coach will be so impressed with her that he and his wife will adopt her.

Planet Earth is Blue by Nicole Panteleakos (2019)

Key issues: Twice-exceptional students; having a passion; supportive siblings

Description: Nova, a 12-year-old, is excited about the upcoming launch of the space shuttle Challenger. It's the first time a teacher is going up into space and kids across the country will watch the event on live television. Nova and her older sister Bridget share a love of astronomy and the space program. They planned to watch the launch together, but Bridget has disappeared, and Nova has to move to another new foster home. While foster families and teachers dismiss Nova as autistic and nonverbal, Bridget understands how smart and special Nova really is. As the liftoff draws closer, Nova's new foster family and teachers begin to recognize her potential. As each day passes, Nova is counting down to the launch and the moment when Bridget will return.

Come Sing, Jimmy Jo by Katherine Paterson (1995)

Key issues: Musical giftedness; peer relationships; individuality

Description: Jimmy Jo is a gifted young musician who must deal with increasing recognition from his audiences as well as problems with his peers.

The Great Gilly Hopkins by Katherine Paterson (2007)

Key issues: Coming of age; relationships with others

Description: Gilly Hopkins, a foster child, yearns desperately for a real family and a place to call home. In her struggle to escape from her foster home, she learns that life usually isn't the way it is supposed to be.

Bridge to Terabithia by Katherine Paterson (2007)

Key issues: Peer relationships; coping skills; dealing with the death of a loved one; creativity

Description: A young man can be "different" much more easily if he has a friend with whom he can share his thoughts and feelings.

A Good Kind of Trouble by Lisa Moore Ramée (2019)

Key issues: Changing friendships; maintaining a value system

Description: Shayla has always been one to follow the rules. She hopes to survive seventh grade with her friendships not changing and learning to run track, but in junior high, all the rules have changed. She is forced to question who her best friends are, and some kids are now saying that she's not Black enough. Shayla's older sister is involved in Black Lives Matter, but Shay doesn't think that's for her. After experiencing a powerful protest, Shay decides some rules are worth breaking and she wears a black armband in support of the Black Lives movement. Soon everyone at school is taking sides and Shayla must remain true to herself.

Ghost by Jason Reynolds (2016)

Key issues: Finding a place where you belong; support of the community to channel talent and energy

Description: Castle "Ghost" Crenshaw has been running for all the wrong reasons. He's been running from the memory of one traumatic life-changing event with his father. Since then, he's been the kid causing problems at school, until he meets Coach, an ex-Olympic medalist who sees natural talent in him and provides him a place on an elite track team. Can Ghost harness his raw talent for speed or will the events of his past control him?

As Brave as You by Jason Reynolds (2017)
Key issues: Fear and bravery; guilt and forgiveness
Description: Genie and Ernie, two brothers from Brooklyn, go to spend the summer with their grandparents in rural Virginia where much will be different: no cell phone reception, daily chores, and getting to know their grandparents. Ernie, the older brother is brave, confident, and cool. Genie is intellectual, often anxious, and afraid. The brothers soon learn that their grandfather is blind. Fascinated by how he matches his clothes, cooks with a gas stove, and pours a glass of sweet tea without spilling it, Genie decides that Grandpop is the bravest man he's ever known. He notices that his grandfather never leaves the house and often disappears into a room filled with songbirds and plants and begins to wonder if his grandfather is so brave after all. When Ernie turns 14, Grandpop decides that in order to be a man, Ernie must learn to shoot a gun. Ernie has no interest in learning. Dumbfounded by his brother's reluctance, Genie reflects on the meaning of being brave. Is bravery becoming a man by proving something or is it more important to own up to what you refuse to do?

Someday Angeline by Louis Sachar (1994)
Key issues: Multipotentiality; prodigies; image management; peer relationships
Description: Angeline is an eight-year-old who has been accelerated to sixth grade, and she must deal with the social issues of "being too smart." The mean kids in school call her a freak, her teacher finds her troublesome, and even her father doesn't know how to handle a gifted girl. Angeline doesn't want to be a freak or genius – she just wants to be herself.

The Wednesday Wars by Gary D. Schmidt (2009)
Key issues: Gifted boys handling family expectations; bullies

Description: Holling Hoodhood is supposed to stay out of seventh-grade trouble because his father's business image can't be tarnished. Holling has a knack for often finding himself in awkward situations like letting the classroom's pet rats escape into the school's duct-work. When his teacher assigns him to read Shakespeare on his own time, he finds that Shakespeare has much to teach him.

A Taste of Blackberries by Doris Buchanan Smith (2004)
Key issues: Coping with death; peer relationships
Description: A touching story about a young boy who deals with the tragic death of his best friend.

The Secret Sheriff of Sixth Grade by Jordan Sonnenblick (2019)
Key issues: Bullying; overcoming dysfunctional families; sensitivity and empathy in adolescence
Description: It's tough being Maverick Falconer, a boy with a difficult homelife and the shortest student in sixth grade. Maverick struggles hard to find friends and is constantly tormented by the athletes in his school. He faces the cruelest of situations but maintains his compassion for others. In memory of his deceased father who left him a toy sheriff's badge that he carries with him at all times, he is determined to make school a better place for everyone.

Maniac Magee by Jerry Spinelli (1999)
Key issues: Being labeled "different"; leadership; relationships with others; positive role models
Description: A boy is so incredibly energetic that "he must be a maniac." He uses his energy and gifts to confront the racial divide in his town that no one else has had the strength to face.

Loser by Jerry Spinelli (2003)
Key issues: Self-acceptance; celebrating individual differences; optimism
Description: Donald Zinkoff is a quirky kid who enjoys people, loves school, and giggles constantly. Other fourth graders think he's a loser. Donald's optimism and energy, combined with his family's love, do not allow him to think of himself that way. When he tries to

rescue a lost child in a winter blizzard, others see the loser become a hero.

Smiles to Go by Jerry Spinelli (2008)

Key issues: Friendships; teenagers searching for self-actualization

Description: Will Tuppence's life has always been driven by rules of science and logic. When he discovers in ninth-grade science class that protons decay, he begins to look at the world differently and develops a new perspective on the important relationships in his life.

Surviving the Applewhites by Stephanie S. Tolan (2002)

Key issues: Underachievement; creativity; relationships with others; image management

Description: When Jake Semple is kicked out of his latest school, the Applewhites, an eccentric family of artists, offer to have him move in with them and attend their unstructured Creative Academy. Through his new family life, Jake explores interests and discovers talents he never knew he had.

Paperboy by Vince Vawter (2013)

Key issues: Self-discovery and acceptance in adolescence; living with a speech impediment

Description: Vince Vauter delivers an autobiographical novel in telling the story of Victor, an 11-year-old boy who stutters. When his best friend Rat visits his grandparents, Victor takes over his paper route. He is introduced to the daily lives of the paper route customers and in reflecting on their challenges, he learns that what he says is more important than how he says it. Victor discovers that his soul doesn't stutter.

The Unsung Hero of Birdsong, USA by Brenda Wood (2019)

Key issues: Learning to look at life through multiple perspectives; friendships that defy age; gender and race; the corrosive effects of racism

Description: For Gabriel Haberlin, life is pretty close to perfect in his small town of Birdsong, South Carolina. On his 12th birthday, his point of view changes when he is struck by a car while riding his new bicycle – an accident that might have been tragic if

Mr. Meriweather Hunter hadn't suddenly appeared and pushed him out of harm's way. Following the accident, young Gabriel and Meriweather become friends when they both start working at Gabriel's father's auto shop. Gabriel uncovers a secret about his new friend: he served in the army's all-Black 761st Tank Battalion in World War II. He learns why it's so dangerous for Meriweather to talk about his heroism in the war in the company of White people. Through this important friendship, Gabriel's eyes are open to the ugly truth about the Jim Crow South, and his understanding of what it means to be a hero is forever changed.

Locomotion by Jacqueline Woodson (2003)

Key issues: Poetry as catharsis; love of family; overcoming adversity and developing resilience

Description: Through a collection of poems, 11-year-old Lonnie Collins Motion, nicknamed Locomotion, writes about the death of his parents in a fire, being separated from his younger sister, living in a foster home, and finding his voice through poetry.

Peace, Locomotion by Jacqueline Woodson (2009)

Key issues: Love of family; overcoming adversity and developing resilience; writing as catharsis

Description: Through writing letters to his younger sister living in a different foster home in Brooklyn, Lonnie maintains a record of their lives while they are apart. In his poignant reflections, he expresses his love for his sister, shares his own foster family, and describes his experiences watching his foster brother return home from the Iraq war.

Young Adult Literature: Middle and High School

The Poet X by Elizabeth Acevedo (2018)

Key issues: Challenges facing culturally diverse gifted young women; finding one's voice

Description: Xiomara Batista feels squelched in her Harlem neighborhood. She has much she wants to express, and she pours her frustration and passion into a leather notebook, reciting the words like prayers. With her mother's insistence that she obeys the teachings of the church, Xiomara realizes that she has to keep her thoughts to herself. So when she's invited to join the school's slam poetry club, she doesn't know how she could attend without her mother finding out, but she simply can't stop thinking about performing her poems. In a world that may not want to hear her, Xiomara cannot remain silent.

The Crossover by Kwame Alexander (2019)

Key issues: Supportive sibling relationships; grieving the loss of a loved one

Description: Josh and Jordan Bell are twin brothers, and both are kings on the court thanks to their dad who has invested so much time nurturing their talents. As the winning season unfolds, the twins' bond changes when Jordan develops a serious crush and begins to lose focus. Tensions between the brothers rise. Josh is concerned about both his brother and his father, the number one man in his life. When dad suffers a fatal heart attack, Josh and Jordan reconcile their differences and work through their grief together. (This novel is delivered in dynamic poetic verse.)

Posted by John David Anderson (2018)

Key issues: Bullying; social media; broken friendships

Description: When cell phones are banned at Branton Middle School, Frost and his friends come up with a new way to communicate, leaving sticky notes for each other all around the school. It catches on and soon all the kids in school are leaving notes. For every kind note delivered, there is a cruel and abusive one as well. In the midst of this, a new girl named Rose arrives and joins Frost at his lunch table. Rose is unlike any other girl at Branton and it soon becomes clear that the close circle of friends Frost has made for himself won't easily hold another. As the sticky-note war escalates, the pressure to choose sides mounts and Frost realizes that nothing will ever be the same.

Speak by Laurie Halse Anderson (2006)

Key issues: Coping with trauma; image management; underachievement

Description: A creative high school student's world has been shattered so much so that she can no longer speak. A story of perseverance in the face of trauma.

Me, Earl and the Dying Girl by Jesse Andrews (2012)

Key issues: Loyalty in friendship; using your talents to support those in need; identity

Description: Greg Gaines has managed to survive most of high school by staying on the periphery of his school's social environment. He has only one friend, Earl, and together they spend their time making movies. When Greg's mother mandates that he rekindle a childhood friendship with Rachel who has been diagnosed with leukemia, Greg is forced to abandon invisibility and position himself in the spotlight. When Rachel stops treatment, Greg and Earl decide to create a film for her, a project that becomes a turning point in each of their lives.

Nothing but the Truth by Avi (2010)

Key issues: Gender role expectations; being labeled "different"; relationships with others; underachievement

Description: Philip's teacher wants him to have the same passion for literature as he does for track, but he just doesn't connect to the assigned reading material. When his behavior is viewed as disrespectful and unpatriotic by the teacher, Philip decides to stand up for his rights and ends up in the midst of a national debate.

The Story of Arthur Truluv by Elizabeth Berg (2017)

Key issues: Friendships in unlikely places; celebrating sensitivity and empathy

Description: Arthur Moses is widowed. Each and every day he tends to his rose garden and his cat, then travels to the cemetery to visit his beloved late wife for lunch. Maddy Harris visits the cemetery to escape the kids in her high school. She joins Arthur and a beautiful friendship begins. Moved by Arthur's kindness and devotion, Maddy nicknames him "Truluv." When Arthur's neighbor Lucille enters their circle, the three come together and through heartache and hardships, help one another rediscover their own potential.

The Epic Fail of Arturo Zamora by Pablo Cartaya (2018)

Key issues: Family pride; remaining true to one's value system; identity development

Description: For 13-year-old Arturo Zamora, summer in Miami usually means playing basketball until dark, sipping mango smoothies, and hanging out with friends. This summer involves working in his abuela's restaurant, surviving his first crush, battling an unscrupulous land developer from taking over his neighborhood, and saving the family's business. Can Arturo do it all or is he in for a big epic fail?

American Panda by Gloria Chao (2018)

Key issues: Identity development in gifted females; living up to family expectations

Description: At 17, Mei is a freshman at MIT on track to fulfill the predetermined future her parents have established: become a doctor, marry a preapproved Taiwanese Ivy Leaguer, and deliver many grandchildren. With all that her parents have given up to make her comfortable life a reality, she cannot bring herself to tell the truth: she hates germs, falls asleep in biology lectures, and has a crush on Darren Takahashi, who is certainly not Taiwanese. When she reconnects with her older brother who is estranged from the family for dating the wrong woman, Mei begins to question if all her secrets are truly worth it. Can she find a way to be herself?

The Surprising Power of a Good Dumpling by Wai Chim (2019)

Key issues: Family mental illness; cultural expectations for Asian students

Description: Anna Chiu's life is complicated. When she's not looking after her brother and sister and helping out at her father's restaurant, she's watching over her mother, whose debilitating mental illness keeps her in bed for days. Her father's new delivery boy, Rory, is a welcome distraction, and although she knows things aren't right at home, she's starting to feel like she could be a normal teen. When her mother finally emerges from her bedroom, the situation worsens. As her mother's condition deteriorates, Anna and her family question everything they understand about themselves and each other.

Echoes of the White Giraffe by Sook Nyul Choi (2007)

Key issues: Gender role expectations; multicultural learners; image management

Description: Sookan, a young Korean woman coming of age during the Korean War, experiences a forbidden romance with a quiet, thoughtful young man who allows her to think for herself and challenges aspects of a strict society.

Walk Two Moons by Sharon Creech (2019)

Key issues: Peer relationships; family relationships; image management

Description: After her mother leaves the family, Sal embarks upon a weeklong trip with her grandparents during which she tells the story of how she became close with someone who at first seemed utterly unlike herself.

Bloomability by Sharon Creech (2012)

Key issues: Family relationships; culturally diverse learners

Description: Dinnie spends a year away from her family while attending an international school in Switzerland. With time away from her transient family, she discovers an expanding world and finds her place in it. In her new environment, she learns that life is full of new "bloomabilities."

Chasing Redbird by Sharon Creech (2012)

Key issues: Family relationships; coping with death; introversion; image management; heightened sensitivity

Description: Zinny is one of seven kids and often escapes the hustle and bustle of her family by going to the quiet house of her aunt and uncle. When her aunt dies, Zinny thinks it's her fault. She ends up dealing with her feelings during the summer as she clears a long-overgrown trail that parallels her emotions.

Ironman by Chris Crutcher (2004)

Key issues: Athletic giftedness; family relationships; image management; coping skills

Description: Triathlete Bo's rocky relationship with his English teacher is frustratingly similar to what remains of his relationship with his father. With the help of sports, an anger management group, and writing, Bo learns to cope.

The Watsons Go to Birmingham – 1963 by Christopher Paul Curtis (2013)

Key issues: Family relationships; being alone; image management

Description: Kenny, a gifted boy in 1960s America, spends his time trying to avoid teasing from bullies and his tough older brother, Byron. The family thinks a summer in Birmingham may be what Byron needs to learn to behave, but they learn some lessons about racial barriers and institutionalized bullying instead.

We Were Here by Matt de la Pena (2009)

Key issues: Reaching self-understanding and acceptance; moral development

Description: Following his crime, the judge sentences Miguel to a year in a group home where he is required to write a journal so his counselor can figure out how he thinks. Miguel realizes that the judge has actually done him a favor. In the group home, Miguel connects with two other boys who together escape from the home and plan their return to Mexico where they can start over. Through this journey, Miguel discovers that running away is the quickest path right back to what he is running from.

Whirligig by Paul Fleischman (2001)

Key issues: Relationships with others; image management; coping skills; dealing with tragedy

Description: Popularity-obsessed Brent's quest for a higher social ranking eventually leads to the death of an 18-year-old girl. At the girl's mother's request, Brent begins a journey of atonement that takes him to the corners of the country and into people's lives that will be forever tied with his.

Seedfolks by Paul Fleischman (2014)

Key issues: Appreciating cultural diversity; building community

Description: An urban vacant lot looked like no place for a garden, especially for a neighborhood of neighbors where no one appears to care. A young girl clears a small space and digs into the hard-packed soil to plant her precious bean seeds. The soil holds great promise: to Curtis who believes he can win back Lateesha's heart with a harvest of tomatoes; to Virgil's father who sees a fortune to be made from growing lettuce; and even to Mariclea, a pregnant teenager who dreads motherhood. Through 13 different voices, the author tells the story of a garden that transformed a neighborhood.

Perfect by Natasha Friend (2004)

Key issues: Eating disorders in talented young women; the pressure to be outwardly perfect

Description: For Isabelle Lee, whose father recently died, everything appears normal on the outside, but everything is not okay. Her family no longer functions and she's struggling with loneliness. She tries to cope by binging and purging. When she is sent to a group counseling session, she is stunned to see that Ashley Barnum, the prettiest most together girl in school is also attending. As the two girls become friends, they learn together that nobody is perfect.

If I Ever Get Out of Here by Eric Gansworth (2013)

Key issues: Cross-cultural friendship; poverty; racism; bullying

Description: Lewis "Shoe" Blake is bright, poor, and scrawny and the only kid from the Tuscarora Reservation tracked with the "brainiacs" at their county middle school in upstate New York. During sixth grade, Lewis was invisible, but when rugged George Haddonfield arrives at the Air Force base and shows up in seventh grade, Lewis finds his first real friend. The boys bond over music and slowly let their guards down. When Evan Reininger, a well-connected bully sets his sights on Lewis, the friendship between George and Lewis friendship undergoes a true test.

The Remarkable Journey of Coyote Sunrise by Dan Gemeinhart (2019)

Key issues: Resilience; gifted girls taking charge of life's challenges

Description: Since the loss of her mother and two sisters in a car accident, Coyote and her father have lived on the road in an old school bus, traveling throughout the country. When she learns that the park in her old neighborhood is to be demolished – the same park where she, her mother, and her sisters buried a treasured box of mementos, she implements a plan to get her father to drive 3,600 miles to reclaim the memory box. Along the way, they pick up a crew of misfit travelers who help them to work through their grief.

The Curious Incident of the Dog in the Night-Time by Mark Haddon (2004)

Key issues: Twice-exceptionality; family relationships; relationships with others; image management; coping skills

Description: A highly gifted student with learning disabilities embarks upon a series of adventures to figure out how his neighbor's dog was killed, learning family secrets and important things about himself along the way.

The Planet of Junior Brown by Virginia Hamilton (2006)

Key issues: Image management; artistic giftedness; musical giftedness; relationships with others

Description: Overweight and gifted in the arts, Junior has trouble making real connections with others. Through his relationship with fellow student Buddy, Junior is better able to accept himself and learn to be closer with others.

Hoot by Carl Hiaasen (2005)

Key issues: Being labeled "different"; leadership

Description: Roy Eberhardt is the new kid in school once again. He faces the same routine: eating alone at lunch, no real friends, and bullies pushing him around. He connects with bully beating Beatrice and together they become involved in another student's attempt to save a colony of burrowing owls from a proposed construction site.

When Zachary Beaver Came to Town by Kimberly Willis Holt (2001)

Key issues: Peer relationships; being labeled "different"

Description: When Zachary Beaver, an obese teenager, arrives in a small Texas town as part of a traveling road show, Toby and his friends become fascinated with him and the stories he shares of all the places he's known. In coming to know Zachary, Toby learns to appreciate the boy's difficult life as he develops sensitivity to people who are different from him.

The Next Great Paulie Fink by Lynda Mullaly Hunt (2013)

Key issues: Identity development; reaching self-understanding and acceptance

Description: Caitlyn Breen begins a puzzling new life at Mitchell School, where students take care of real live goats and actually study philosophers. She soon learns that nobody there can stop talking about a boy named Paulie Fink. To some, Paulie was a hilarious class clown, a troublemaker, a hapless klutz, or a genius. One thing is certain: Paulie Fink was legendary. Now he has disappeared and Caitlyn finds herself in charge of a reality show competition to discover the school's next great Paulie Fink. With each challenge she faces, Caitlyn struggles to understand this person she never met, but in the process, what she learns about herself is most surprising.

One for the Murphys by Lynda Mullaly Hunt (2013)

Key issues: Resilience in childhood; learning to trust others

Description: Carley uses her sharp sense of humor and street smarts to maintain her strong emotional walls. When she becomes a foster child and moves in with the Murphys, she is overwhelmed. Her new loving family shows her the family life she never knew, and she struggles to understand her new household. Although she resists, the Murphys eventually show her what it feels like to belong, until her mother wants her back and Carley must decide where and how to live. She's not a Murphy, but the gifts they have given Carley have helped her accept her future.

We Regret to Inform You: An Overachiever's Guide to College Rejection by Ariel Kaplan (2018)

Key issues: Identity development in high-achieving students; the pressure of college admission

Description: Mischa, a senior at Blanchard High, is the model student behind the perfectly well-rounded college application. When she is rejected by the Ivies and her safety school, she is devastated. All the sacrifices her single mother made to send her to prep school, the long nights cramming for exams, and the résumé boosting extracurricular activities amount to nothing. When she discovers that her transcript was hacked, she connects with a group of high school techies to launch an investigation that rocks the quiet community of Blanchard Prep. Through Mischa's experience, Blanchard students are reminded that they are more than their GPA and test scores.

Deacon Locke Went to Prom by Brian Katcher (2017)

Key issues: Identity development; loyalty in friendship; the role of social media in adolescent life; coping with loved ones with dementia; challenging xenophobia

Description: Deacon Locke is an awkward high school senior who doesn't think he can get a date for the prom and decides to take his best friend, his grandmother, as his date. He prepares for prom by taking dance lessons from Soraya, a beautiful girl unlike any other he's ever met. He stumbles into accidental fame when a video of him and his prom date goes viral. From then on, Deacon's life with his grandmother, Soraya, and high school peers becomes more complex than he could have ever imagined.

Somewhere Between Bitter and Sweet by Laeken Zea Kemp (2021)

Key issues: Familial expectations; finding where you belong; overcoming adversity

Description: Penelope Prado has always dreamed of opening her own bakery next to her father's restaurant, Nacho's Tacos. However, her parents insist that she pursues a degree in nursing. When they discover that she has been skipping classes, they fire her from the restaurant and let her know that she can only remain at home if she finishes school. Xander Amaro has been searching for home since he was a boy. For him, a job at Nacho's Tacos is his chance at a normal life, to settle in at his abuelo's, and to find his father who left him behind. When the restaurant and Xander's immigrant status are threatened, he must do everything he can to protect his newfound family. Together, he and Penelope navigate their relationship, discover where they belong, and preserve the place they call home.

If I Love You, Am I Trapped Forever? by M. E. Kerr (2011)

Key issues: Peer and parental expectations; multipotentiality; coping skills

Description: A handsome, multitalented, and popular young man has a great deal of pressure placed on him with expectations from his high school friends, parents, and self. He struggles to maintain his image.

The Outcasts of 19 Schuyler Place by E. L. Konigsburg (2004)

Key issues: Artistic giftedness; creativity; image management; being labeled "different"; relationships with others

Description: Margaret's tendency not to bow to authority gets her kicked out of summer camp. With her parents out of the country, she ends up at her eccentric uncle's house, which is well known in the area for the huge sculptures in the yard. The town starts a movement to get rid of the structures, and soon Margaret's summer gets much more serious and meaningful.

Schooled by Gordon Korman (2007)

Key issues: Being labeled "different"; celebrating individual differences; peer relationships

Description: Cap Anderson is being home schooled by his grandmother on a commune. When his grandmother is hospitalized, he is forced to attend a public middle school where the students maintain a tradition of voting for the dorkiest kid in school to be president of eighth grade. With his lack of social understanding, Cap is bullied and elected class president. Several events occur in which Cap's sensitivity to the needs of others serves him well and he emerges as a hero to the student body.

Very Far Away from Anywhere Else by Ursula K. Le Guin (2004)

Key issues: Introversion; peer relationships; image management; nonconformity

Description: Owen Griffiths tells his story of being a "bright little jerk" and how he deals with being different. He has discovered that conforming for the sake of conformity will not work for him, although he is not yet comfortable being himself. Owen learns from Natalie, and when their friendship shows signs of turning into love, he learns even more about taking charge of his future.

The Giver by Lois Lowry (2006)

Key issues: Underachievement; image management; nonconformity

Description: Twelve-year-old Jonas has been taken under the wing of "The Giver," his utopian society's keeper of all secrets and memories. He must learn to balance his search for identity with his community's wishes for him as he decides if he will fulfill the role society has laid out for him.

Sleeping Freshmen Never Lie by David Lubar (2007)

Key issues: Image management; surviving the first year of high school; friendships that change

Description: As Scott Hudson navigates his first year of high school, he awaits the birth of a new baby brother. He decides that high school would be less overwhelming if it came with a survival manual, so he writes his reflections and provides a guide of survival tips for his new sibling.

The Facts and Fictions of Minna Pratt by Patricia MacLachlan (2002)

Key issues: Image management; family relationships; musical giftedness; creativity

Description: Minna is surrounded by gifted people: her mother is an author, her father is a psychologist, her younger brother "knows everything," and she plays in a quartet of very talented musicians. She learns to value her family because of their eccentricities and to value herself because of her own.

A Very Large Expanse of Sea by Tahereh Mafi (2018)

Key issues: Identity; race and Islamophobia; stereotypes; cross-cultural friendships and first love

Description: A year after the events of 9/11, Shirin has transferred to yet another high school. It's a turbulent time for society, and for a highly intelligent 16-year-old Muslim girl who confronts stereotyping daily, it is emotionally exhausting. Shirin endures rude stares, degrading comments, and physical violence as a result of her race, her religion, and the hijab she wears every day. She doesn't trust anyone, and she doesn't even try to fit in anywhere or let others close enough to hurt her. She copes with her frustrations through music and spends her afternoons breakdancing with her older brother. But then she meets Ocean Desmond James, the first person who seems to really want to get to know Shirin. This terrifies her as they seem to come from two irreconcilable worlds. Shirin has protected herself emotionally for so long she is unsure as to how to negotiate this significant relationship.

Jeremy Fink and the Meaning of Life by Wendy Mass (2006)
Key issues: Son-father relationships; search for self-actualization
Description: Just before his 13th birthday Jeremy Fink receives a key-less locked box, prepared by his father before his death five years earlier. According to the writing on the box, it contains the meaning of life. How will he open the box and what will he discover?

Cut by Patricia McCormick (2002)
Key issues: Perfectionism; image management; being alone
Description: Burdened with the pressure of believing she is responsible for her brother's illness, 15-year-old Callie begins a course of self-destruction that leads to her being admitted to a psychiatric hospital. Slowly, she begins emerging from her miserable silence, ultimately understanding the role her dysfunctional family played in her brother's health crisis.

The Member of the Wedding by Carson McCullers (2004)
Key issues: Family relationships; image management; being alone
Description: Tomboy Frankie yearns to experience more than her small town will offer her; she thinks she has found the perfect solution when her older brother gets married and asks Frankie to be a "member of the wedding." Frankie misunderstands and thinks she'll be accompanying the couple from now on, and when she realizes her mistake, she must reevaluate herself.

Hurricane Season by Nicole Melleby (2019)
Key issues: Bipolar disorder; coming out; developing resilience
Description: Fig loves her father and the home they share in a beach-side community. She is navigating the challenges of middle school while taking care of her dad, a famous musician whose mental health has deteriorated over time. In her attempt to understand him, she immerses herself in the biographies of Vincent Van Gogh, an artist whose temperament reminds her of her father's. In doing so, will she perhaps unlock his secrets?

Slay by Brittney Morris (2019)

Key issues: Racial identity development; bullying in a virtual world

Description: Kiera Johnson is a senior honors student and one of the only Black students at Jerrson Academy. At home, she joins thousands of Black gamers who duel worldwide as Nubian personas in the secret multiplayer online role-playing card game, SLAY. No one knows that Kiera is the game developer, including her boyfriend Malcolm, who believes video games are partially responsible for "the downfall of the Black man." When a teenager is murdered over a dispute in the SLAY world, news of the game hits the mainstream media and is seen as racist. Determined to save the only world in which she can be herself, Kiera must preserve her secret identity and come to grips with what it means to be unapologetically Black in a world intimidated by Blackness.

Hoops by Walter Dean Myers (1989)

Key issues: Culturally diverse learners; image management; athletic giftedness

Description: While growing up on the streets of Harlem, Lonnie Jackson, a talented athlete, finds basketball more than just a sure way out of the city. Through the game, he gains the confidence to deal with everyday realities.

Game by Walter Dean Myers (2009)

Key issues: Facing pressure to excel; athletic giftedness

Description: Drew Lawson realizes that basketball has to take him places because his academic record certainly won't. His plan runs into trouble when his coach's new offense has made another teammate a star. As the team makes the playoffs, Drew has to come up with a strategy to save his fading college prospects. It's up to him to find out how deep his game really is.

Mike by Andrew Norriss (2019)

Key issues: Living up to parental expectations; journey of self-discovery

Description: Fifteen-year-old Floyd's whole life has revolved around tennis. Since he was a toddler, his father has been preparing him to compete at Wimbledon at a record age. When a mysterious guy named Mike begins showing up at his practices, Floyd is more than annoyed, especially when he discovers that no one else can see or hear Mike. Thus begins Floyd's work with Dr. Pinner, a psychologist, who helps him realize just who Mike might be.

Jacob Have I Loved by Katherine Paterson (2007)
Key issues: Image management; family relationships

Description: Louise is convinced that everyone despises her and loves Caroline, her beautiful, musically talented younger sister. Not until she is 17 does Louise realize that she is gifted intellectually and capable of doing anything she chooses.

The Island by Gary Paulsen (2006)
Key issues: Image management; being alone; search for identity

Description: A young man needs his personal space throughout adolescence as he struggles to "find himself."

Dancing Carl by Gary Paulsen (2007)
Key issues: Heightened sensitivity; gender role stereotypes; athletic giftedness

Description: A stranger new to a small Minnesota community has a great impact on the lives of two 12-year-old boys when he expresses his inner feelings through ice-skating.

The Car by Gary Paulsen (2006)
Key issues: Developing one's independence; problem solving in gifted boys; developing self-understanding; developing resilience to overcome adversity

Description: Terry, a 14-year-old, is abandoned by his parents. He travels west in search of his uncle in a car he built himself. Along the way, he picks up two Vietnam veterans, learns from their experiences, and ultimately learns about himself.

The Seventh Most Important Thing by Shelley Pearsall (2016)
Key issues: Grieving the loss of a loved one; shaping our perceptions of others;

Description: Arthur, a seventh grader, is mad at the world. Even though his recently deceased father was far from perfect, Arthur grieves for his loss, and he's not ready to forgive his mother for tossing out his dad's belongings. He's furious at the raggedy old Junk Man wearing his dad's favorite hat, so he grabs a brick and throws it at the trash picker. The Junk Man survives the violent act and intervenes with the judge who commits Arthur to community service working for The Junk Man, an artist and collector of interesting objects. Arthur is given a shopping cart and a list of the Seven Most Important Things he must acquire. In his search for the seven items, he reaches self-understanding and redemption.

Charming as a Verb by Ben Philippe (2020)

Key issues: First-generation racial and class struggles for teenagers; moral and ethical dilemmas

Description: Henri Haltiwanger is both determined and charming. As a first-generation scholarship student at his private high school, he has become a star debater and popular personality. His cultivated suaveness and confident persona are evident as he's created a dog-walking business disguised as a much larger corporation to lure wealthy New York clients into trusting him with their pets. Henri hopes this hustle will help him achieve his dream of getting into Columbia University. There is only one person who is immune to Henri's charms: his socially awkward classmate and neighbor Corrine Troy. When she discovers Henri's approach to his dog-walking enterprise, she blackmails him into improving her social standings so she will look better on her application to Princeton. What happens will alter the trajectory of their lives.

The Boy in the Black Suit by Jason Reynolds (2015)

Key issues: Overcoming the loss of a parent; dealing with grief; resilience

Description: Seventeen-year-old Matt wears a black suit every day. Not because his mother died but because he has a new gig at the local funeral home, which pays much more than working at Cluck Bucket. He needs the money since his grief-stricken father can't handle the bills or anything else. When Matt meets Lovey, a girl who has been through more challenges than he can imagine, he sees that she never cries. Lovey is tough, really tough. Tough in the way Matt wishes he could be. Matt is attracted to her and discovers there is nothing more hopeful than finding a friend who understands your loneliness and can maybe even take it away.

All American Boys by Jason Reynolds and Brendan Kiely (2017)

Key issues: Racial profiling and police brutality; loyalty in friendship

Description: Two teens, one Black and one White, grapple with the repercussions of a single violent act that leaves their school, their community, and eventually, the country divided by racial tension. As the events become explosive, best friends are forced to face decisions and consequences that they had never considered before.

I Am Not Your Perfect Mexican Daughter by Erika Sanchez (2019)

Key issues: Supporting giftedness in culturally diverse young women; grieving the loss of a loved one; resilience

Description: Perfect Mexican daughters never abandon their family. They do not leave their parents' house after high school and go off to college. But Julia is not perfect. That role belonged to her older sister Olga. When a tragic accident takes Olga's life, Julia is left behind to reassemble the shattered pieces of her family; however, no one seems to realize that Julia is also broken. After her sister's death. Julia discovers that Olga might not have been the perfect young woman everybody admired. Julia is determined to find out and in doing so she begins to understand who she is as a talented female.

The Beginning of Everything by Robyn Schneider (2013)

Key issues: New beginnings that stem from adversity

Description: Varsity tennis captain Ezra Faulkner was supposed to be homecoming king, but that was yesterday – before his girlfriend cheated on him, before a car accident shattered his leg, and before he fell in love with unpredictable new girl Cassidy Thorpe. As he copes with his challenges and discovers who his true friends are, Ezra works hard to determine just who he is and reaches an understanding of how adversity can change an individual in positive ways.

You Asked for Perfect by Laura Silverman (2019)

Key issues: Perfectionism and stress in gifted teenagers; academic competition among peers; parental expectations; identity development; gifted males negotiating a gay relationship

Description: Ariel Stone is a high school senior who has dedicated his adolescence to cultivating the perfect résumé for Harvard: first chair violinist, dedicated volunteer, active synagogue congregant, and expected valedictorian. In a community where academic pressure on stressed teens could not be higher, Amir barely considers having a social life, let alone a relationship. When a poor grade on a calculus quiz places his future on the line, Ariel is forced to enlist a classmate, Amir, as a tutor. As the two spend time together, Ariel discovers he may not like calculus, but he does like Amir. When he's with Amir, the academic pressure fades away and a more positive attitude about life emerges. As college deadlines are looming, adding a new relationship to a lengthy list of commitments may push Ariel past his limit.

Counting by 7s by Holly Goldberg Sloan (2013)
Key issues: Coping with loss; resilience
Description: Willow Chance is a highly gifted young woman obsessed with nature and diagnosing medical conditions. She struggles to connect with others and finds it comforting to count by 7s. When she loses her adoptive parents in a tragic car accident, she is alone in a world that becomes overwhelming. Her journey to discover a supportive surrogate family enables her to push through her grief and overcome her loss.

Notes from the Midnight Driver by Jordan Sonnenblick (2006)
Key issues: Coping with divorce; mentoring relationships
Description: Alex Gregory is a 16-year-old who is furious over his parents' divorce. When he gets into a car accident and is charged for driving under the influence, the judge requires him to pay for the damages and work 100 hours of community service at a nursing home. He is assigned to Sol, an angry and lonely old man. In his required weekly visits, Alex decides to play his guitar for Sol. When he discovers that Sol was once a successful jazz guitar player, he receives some important musical training. A warm friendship with Sol evolves and Alex benefits from important life lessons. In gratitude, he recruits other musicians to join him in delivering a benefit concert for the nursing home residents.

Zen and the Art of Faking It by Jordan Sonnenblick (2007)
Key issues: Searching for friendships; popularity; identity development
Description: San Lee is forced to move again to a new community and
a new middle school. He attempts to fit in by becoming known as
the Zen expert of eighth grade. With a little library research and the
perfect "meditation" rock outside his school, San fools everyone
into believing his Buddhist philosophy.

Drums, Girls, and Dangerous Pie by Jordan Sonnenblick (2010)
Key issues: Sensitivity and compassion
Description: Steven has a perfectly normal teenage life. He's a drum-
mer in the All-Star Jazz band, has a crush on the most popular girl
in school, and is constantly annoyed by his five-year-old brother
Jeffrey. When Jeffrey is diagnosed with leukemia, Steven's world is
shattered. He must deal with his brother's illness and his parents'
attempts to keep the family together during this time of crisis.

Falling Over Sideways by Jordan Sonnenblick (2017)
Key issues: Families coping with a tragic health crisis; father-daughter
relationships; developing resilience
Description: Claire's life is filled with middle school challenges. While
she enjoys her quirky ways of negotiating adolescence, she feels
like her life is cursed. She struggles to compete in dance and has to
cope with eighth-grade mean girls, bullies, and an aggravating boy
named Ryder. At home, she has to deal with her older brother who
overshadows her and seems perfect in every way. Then all of these
challenges seem trivial when her fun-loving father experiences a
serious stroke. Claire and her family must cling to each other in
order to support her father in overcoming his challenges.

Taking Sides by Gary Soto (2003)
Key issues: Cultural identity; sportsmanship; self-acceptance
Description: When 14-year-old Lincoln Mendoza and his mother move
from their California barrio to a more affluent White suburb, he
misses his Hispanic friends and his old neighborhood. He feels like
a traitor when he plays basketball for his new school and must
compete against his former classmates. Ultimately, Lincoln learns to

accept challenges in his new environment without compromising his cultural identity.

Stargirl by Jerry Spinelli (2004)

Key issues: Nonconformity; image management

Description: When eccentric Stargirl joins the ranks at Mica High School, her utter ignorance of the social order and genuine affection for everyone throws the whole community for a loop.

Wringer by Jerry Spinelli (2004)

Key issues: Heightened sensitivity; gender role expectations

Description: Palmer's upcoming birthday signifies the time he'll become a wringer, or pigeon killer, at his town's annual Pigeon Day. Palmer doesn't want to play this role, but will he have the courage to stand up for his beliefs?

Smiles to Go by Jerry Spinelli (2009)

Key issues: Learning to overcome life's challenges; finding a place to fit in

Description: Will Tuppence is always in control as he plans everything obsessively, from the stargazing night with his crush, Mi-Su, to the regularly scheduled games of Monopoly with his ninth-grade friends. He's even planned his adulthood career as an astronomer. His life changes when he discovers that protons – the tiny atomic particles that are the building blocks to life – can die. The one thing that was so certain in his world has an expiration date. Will must now begin to consider the uncertainties in his life.

Dear Martin by Nic Stone (2017)

Key issues: Gifted Black males and racial profiling; police brutality

Description: Justyce McAllister is an honor student, captain of the debate team, and headed for an Ivy League school but that doesn't seem to matter. Though he's left his rough neighborhood behind, he can't escape the scorn of his former peers or the attitude of his new prep school classmates. He looks to the teachings of Dr. Martin Luther King Jr. for answers and dedicates journaling time to Dr. King to sort through his feelings. When Justyce and his best friend Manny are stopped by a White off-duty cop for driving with their music turned way up, words are heated and shots are fired. Justyce and his friend are caught in the crosshairs. When the media goes viral, it's Justyce who is under attack.

Jackpot! by Nic Stone (2019)

Key issues: Racism and classism; interracial friendships and romance; identity development; overcoming adversity and building resilience

Description: Rico is a high school senior who, after school and working at the local gas station, rushes home to care for her younger brother. The "good" high school her mom insists she attends is unlikely to lead to college afterward, and friends are in short supply because she's hard-wired to keep people at a distance. When she sells a jackpot-winning lotto ticket at the gas station, she thinks maybe her luck will finally change. With serious help from her handsome, popular, and wealthy classmate Zan, can she track down the ticket holder who hasn't claimed the prize? Will the investigative duo from such different worlds unite or divide? When a medical crisis sends her family into deeper debt than they could have imagined, Rico makes a risky final attempt to get the winning ticket, but fate has a twist in store.

Roll of Thunder, Hear My Cry by Mildred D. Taylor (2002)

Key issues: Image management; culturally diverse learners; perseverance; family relationships

Description: Cassie is a girl raised by a family determined not to surrender their independence or their humanity simply because they are Black. Through her family struggles, Cassie learns to be true to herself.

The Hate U Give by Angie Thomas (2017)

Key issues: Gifted Black males and racial profiling; police brutality

Description: Starr Carter switches between two worlds – the poor, mostly Black neighborhood where she lives and the affluent White prep school that she attends. The difficult balance between these worlds is shattered when she is witness to the fatal shooting of her childhood best friend Khalil at the hands of a White police officer. Khalil was unarmed. Shortly after, Khalil's death is a national headline. As tensions mount, and facing pressure from all sides of her community, Starr must discover her voice and speak out for what is right.

Dicey's Song by Cynthia Voigt (2003)

Key issues: Being labeled "different"; family relationships; perseverance; leadership

Description: Dicey is the oldest daughter in a family abandoned by their mother. Dicey is courageous and independent when she takes charge of her life to remain supportive to those who depend on her.

Izzy, Willy-Nilly by Cynthia Voigt (2005)

Key issues: Image management; peer relationships; perfectionism

Description: A drunk-driving accident leaves pretty, popular Izzy with an amputated leg and a group of friends who no longer know how to connect with her. Through a new friendship with an eccentric classmate, Izzy is able to make the transition back to school and face her new life.

The Runner by Cynthia Voigt (2005)

Key issues: Self-inflicted pressure; athletic giftedness; image management

Description: Bullet Tillerman is a gifted athlete. His story is that of a boy who conquers self-doubt and enters adulthood.

A Solitary Blue by Cynthia Voigt (2003)

Key issues: Parental pressure; perfectionism; family relationships

Description: Jeff's mother, who deserted the family years before, reenters his life and widens the gap between Jeff and his father. This gap is one only truth, love, and friendship can heal.

Sons From Afar by Cynthia Voigt (1996)

Key issues: Family relationships; image management

Description: A search for a father forces two brothers to learn their strengths and weaknesses as well as important knowledge about themselves.

Piecing Me Together by Renée Watson (2017)

Key issues: Mentoring culturally diverse gifted girls; finding one's voice

Description: Jade knows that she has to leave her poor neighborhood if she is to succeed and provide a better life for her mother. She leaves her community each day to attend a private school where she excels academically but feels like an outsider. Following her mother's advice, she takes advantage of every opportunity she is offered and joins Women to Women, a mentorship program for girls. Simply because her mentor is Black and graduated from the same high school does not mean that she understands Jade. She is tired of being singled out as someone who needs help. Jade wants to speak, to create, and to express her joys and sorrows as a talented Black female. Perhaps there are some ways she could show other women about negotiating their world and finding authentic ways to make a difference.

Tadpole by Ruth White (2004)

Key issues: Musical giftedness; family relationships; leadership; image management

Description: Carolina feels lost in a family of talented sisters. When her guitar-playing cousin Tadpole comes for an unexpected visit, Carolina realizes she has talents to unlock while coming to a deeper understanding of human nature.

How to be Remy Cameron by Julian Winters (2019)

Key issues: Identity development in gifted males; LGBTQ challenges

Description: Everyone at Maplewood High knows Remy Cameron. He's the openly gay likable guy who friends, faculty, and fellow students admire for his confidence. The only person who isn't sure about Remy is Remy himself. When assigned to write an authentic essay defining who he is and who he wants to be, Remy embarks on an emotional journey toward reconciling the outward labels people attach to him with the real Remy Cameron within.

The Mozart Season by Virginia Euwer Wolff (2007)

Key issues: Musical giftedness; image management

Description: Allegra Shapiro, a sixth grader, is the youngest violinist in a statewide competition. She spends her summer practicing a Mozart concerto and, through her music, she is able to find many significant conceptions in her world.

Balzhar by Meg Wolitzer (2015)

Key issues: Surviving emotional trauma; depression in gifted teens

Description: Following the death of her boyfriend, Jam Gallahue becomes a student at the Wooden Barn, a therapeutic boarding school in rural Vermont. She is one of five students chosen for a supposedly life-changing class called Special Topics in English that focuses on the works of Sylvia Plath. A journal-writing assignment leads Jam into a mysterious otherworld she and her classmates call Belzhar. It is there that the students' lives are as they thought they were before they suffered their trauma allowing them a place of peace. Through the course of their class, Jam and her peers develop deep friendships as they share their stories of trauma.

If You Come Softly by Jacqueline Woodson (2010)

Key issues: Interracial friendships and love; racism and elitism

Description: Jeremiah leaves his Brooklyn neighborhood each day to attend an elite prep school in Manhattan where few Black students fit in. He meets Ellie, a Jewish girl, and discovers quickly that they fit together. Their worlds are so different, but to them, that's not what matters. All they have to do is convince others that their relationship is right.

Behind You by Jacqueline Woodson (2010)

Key issues: Loss of a loved one; grieving

Description: In this sequel to *If You Come Softly*, Jeremiah is tragically killed and the many people who loved him must learn how to move on in life without him. Through hope, understanding, and love, their healing begins.

Maizon at Blue Hill by Jacqueline Woodson (2002)

Key issues: Culturally diverse learners; identity development; peer relationships

Description: Maizon, a gifted African American girl, leaves her grandmother in Brooklyn, NY, to attend a private school in Connecticut on a scholarship. She must cope with her fear of leaving her grandmother, losing her best friend, and losing her identity in a school with little diversity.

Millicent Min, Girl Genius by Lisa Yee (2003)

Key issues: Accelerated gifted girls coping with social issues; hiding one's intelligence to gain friends

Description: Millie, an 11-year-old, is a highly gifted girl enrolled in a summer college poetry class and waiting for her high school senior year. Because she is socially awkward, her parents sign her up for a volleyball team and enlist her to tutor Stanford Wong, her nemesis. Her volleyball teammate Emily becomes her first true friend, but Millie feels compelled to camouflage her intelligence.

Stanford Wong Flunks Big-Time by Lisa Yee (2006)

Key issues: Underachievement; family expectations; peer group pressure

Description: From the day his father named him for his alma mater, great things were expected of Stanford Wong. When he flunks sixth-grade English class and has to attend summer school, he worries that he might lose his star status on the basketball team. His summer is filled with turmoil as he misses out on basketball camp, he observes his beloved grandmother's increasing dementia, and he has to face being tutored by Millicent Min, girl genius.

The Pigman by Paul Zindel (2005)

Key issues: Learning love, compassion, and trust; identity development; friendships

Description: Coming from unhappy homes, high school sophomores John and Lorraine spend their days in idle pranks. By accident, they meet Angelo Pignati, who is known as "The Pigman." The lonely old man befriends the two teens and through his kindness, they experience more happiness than they've ever had before.

References

Abellán-Pagnini, L., & Hébert, T. P. (2013). Using picture books to guide and inspire young gifted Hispanic students. *Gifted Child Today, 36*(1), 47–56.

Barnes, D. (2017). *Crown: An ode to the fresh cut*. Agate Bolden.

Bishop, R. S. (1990, Summer). Mirrors, windows, and sliding glass doors. *Perspectives: Choosing and Using Books for the Classroom, 6*(3) ix–xi.

Bruker Bradley, K. (2016). *The war that saved my life*. Puffin Books.

Chao, G. (2018). *American panda*. Simon & Schuster.

Cisneros, E. (2020). *Efrén divided*. Quill Tree Books.

Cross, T. L. (2004). *On the social and emotional lives of gifted children: Issues and factors in their psychological development* (2nd ed.). Prufrock Press.

De Vries, D., Brennan, Z., Lankin, M., Morse, R., Rix, B., & Beck, T. (2017). Healing with books: A literature review of bibliotherapy used with children and youth who have experienced trauma. *Therapeutic Recreation Journal, LI*(1), 48–74.

Fears-Floyd, E., & Hébert, T. P. (2010). Using picture book biographies to nurture the talents of young gifted African American students. *Gifted Child Today, 33*(2), 38–46.

Ford, D. Y. (2000). Multicultural literature and gifted Black students: Promoting self-understanding, awareness, and pride. *Roeper Review, 22*(4), 235–240.

Halsted, J. W. (2009). *Some of my best friends are books: Guiding gifted readers from pre-school to high school* (3rd ed.). Great Potential Press.

Hébert, T. P. (2017, May). *Side by side, heart to heart, and hands on* (pp. 5–6). Teaching for High Potential.

Hébert, T. P. (2018). Developing compassion and empathy in gifted students [Conference session]. *South Carolina Region Five Gifted and Talented Education Conference*, North Charleston, SC, United States.

Hébert, T. P. (2019). *Gifted kids facing life with compassion and resilience*. Summer Institute in Gifted Education, Boise State University, Boise, ID, United States.

Hébert, T. P. (2020). *Understanding the social and emotional lives of gifted students* (2nd ed.). Prufrock Academic Press.

Hébert, T. P., & Kent, R. (2000). Nurturing social and emotional development of gifted teenagers through young adult literature. *Roeper Review, 22*(3), 167–171.

Kaplan, A. (2018). *We regret to inform you*. Alfred A. Knopf.

Katcher, B. (2017). *Deacon Locke went to prom*. Katherine Tegen Books.

Lejeune, A. L. (1969, November). Bibliocounseling as a guidance technique. *Catholic Library World, 41*, 156–164.

Lenkowsky, R. S. (1987). Bibliotherapy: A review and analysis of the literature. *The Journal of Special Education, 21*(2), 123–132.

Lundsteen, S. (1972). A thinking improvement program through literature. *Elementary English, 49*(4), 505–512.

Manes, S. (2018). *Be a perfect person in just three days!* Cadwallader & Stearn.

Paulsen, G. (2014). *The island*. Scholastic.

Paulsen, G. (2006). *The car*. Harcourt.

Pett, M., & Rubinstein, G. (2011). *The girl who never made mistakes*. Sourcebooks Jabberwocky.

Pirsig, R. (2006). *Zen and the art of motorcycle maintenance*. Harper Torch.

Polacco, P. (2012). *Thank you, Mr. Falker*. Philomel.

Potok, C. (1987). *The chosen*. Fawcett.

Reynolds, J. (2017). *As brave as you*. Atheneum.

Richards, S. (2021). *Windows, mirrors, and sliding glass doors: Books to include and affirm all identities* [virtual webinar]. Leadership in Diversity, University of Connecticut, Storrs, CT, United States.

Ross, T. (1997). *Eggbert: The slightly cracked egg*. Puffin Books.

Stambaugh, T. (2019). Media and text as framework for meeting the affective needs of gifted and talented students through scaffolding [Paper presentation]. *South Carolina Consortium for Gifted Education Conference*, Columbia, SC, United States.

University of Toronto Press. Books are essential: An update from UTP. March 25, 2020, at 2:03:38 PM Eastern Daylight Time (info@utppublishing.ccsend.com).

Weissberg, R. P., Durlak, J. A., Domitrovich, C. E., & Gullotta, T. P. (2015). Social and emotional learning: Past, present, and future. In J. A. Durlak, C. E. Domitrovich, R. P. Weissberg, & T. P. Gullotta (Eds.). *Handbook of social and emotional learning: Research and practice* (pp. 3–19). The Guilford Press.

Whitcomb, M. (1998). *Odd Velvet*. Chronicle Books.

Woodson, J. (2018). *The day you begin*. Nancy Paulsen Books.

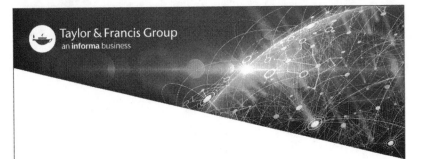